D0357193

SEMINAR STUDIES IN HISTORY

Editor: Patrick Richardson

HENRY VIII

SEMINAR STUDIES IN HISTORY

Editor: Patrick Richardson

A full list of titles in this
series will be found on the
back cover of this book

SEMINAR STUDIES IN HISTORY

HENRY VIII

M. D. Palmer

LONGMAN

LONGMAN GROUP LIMITED
London

ASSOCIATED COMPANIES, BRANCHES AND
REPRESENTATIVES THROUGHOUT THE WORLD

First published 1971

ISBN 0 582 31428 3

PRINTED IN GREAT BRITAIN BY
WESTERN PRINTING SERVICES LTD, BRISTOL

Contents

Contents

Introduction to the Series

The seminar method of teaching is being used increasingly. It is a way of learning in smaller groups through discussion, designed both to get away from and to supplement the basic lecture techniques. To be successful, the members of a seminar must be informed—or else, in the unkind phrase of a cynic—it can be a 'pooling of ignorance'. The chapter in the textbook of English or European history by its nature cannot provide material in this depth, but at the same time the full academic work may be too long and perhaps too advanced.

For this reason we have invited practising teachers to contribute short studies on specialised aspects of British and European history with these special needs in mind.

For this series the authors have been asked to provide, in addition to their basic analysis, a full selection of documentary material of all kinds and an up-to-date and comprehensive bibliography. Both these sections are referred to in the text, but it is hoped that they will prove to be valuable teaching and learning aids in themselves.

Note on the System of References:
A bold number in round brackets (**5**) in the text refers the reader to the corresponding entry in the Bibliography section at the end of the book.

A bold number in square brackets, preceded by 'doc' [**docs 6, 8**] refers the reader to the corresponding items in the section of Documents, which follows the main text.

PATRICK RICHARDSON
General Editor

Acknowledgements

We are grateful to the following for permission to reproduce copyright material:

Cambridge University Press for an extract from *Obedience in Church and State* by Janelle; The Clarendon Press, Oxford, for selections from *Cromwell's Letters* by R. B. Merriman, extracts from *Records of the Reformation* by Nicholas Pocock, 1870, and extracts from *History of the Reformation* by Burnet, edited by N. Pocock; Yale University Press for an extract from *The Life and Death of Cardinal Wolsey* by George Cavendish from *Two Early Tudor Lives* edited by Richard S. Sylvester and Davis P. Harding.

The cover picture is reproduced by permission of the Mansell Collection.

THE HOUSE OF YORK

Richard Plantagenet
duke of York
(d.1460)

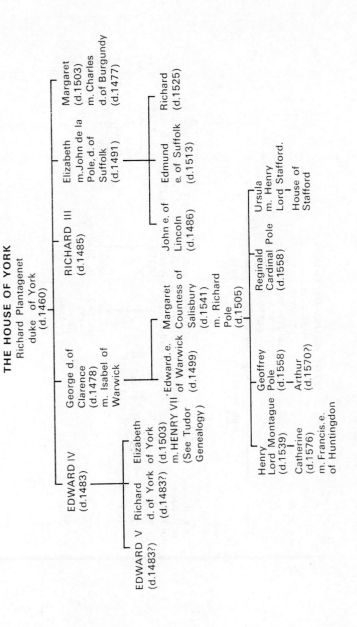

EDWARD IV
(d.1483)

George d.of
Clarence
(d.1478)
m. Isabel of
Warwick

RICHARD III
(d.1485)

Elizabeth
m.John de la
Pole, d. of
Suffolk
(d.1491)

Margaret
(d.1503)
m. Charles
d.of Burgundy
(d.1477)

EDWARD V
(d.1483?)

Richard
d. of York
(d.1483?)

Elizabeth
of York
(d.1503)
m. HENRY VII
(See Tudor
Genealogy)

Edward, e.
of Warwick
(d.1499)

Margaret
Countess of
Salisbury
(d.1541)
m. Richard
Pole
(d.1505)

John e. of
Lincoln
(d.1486)

Edmund
e. of Suffolk
(d.1513)

Richard
(d.1525)

Henry
Lord Montague
(d.1539)

Geoffrey
Pole
(d.1558)

Reginald
Cardinal Pole
(d.1558)

Ursula
m. Henry
Lord Stafford.

House of
Stafford

Catherine
(d.1576)
m. Francis. e.
of Huntingdon

Arthur
(d.1570?)

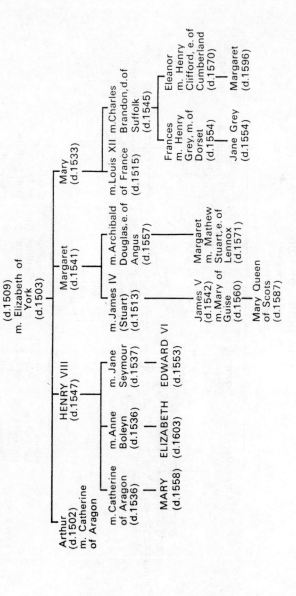

THE HOUSE OF TUDOR

HENRY VII
(d.1509)
m. Elizabeth of
York
(d.1503)

HENRY VIII
(d.1547)

Margaret
(d.1541)

Mary
(d.1533)

Henry VIII's marriages

m.Catherine
of Aragon
(d.1536)

m.Anne
Boleyn
(d.1536)

m. Jane
Seymour
(d.1537)

MARY
(d.1558)

ELIZABETH
(d.1603)

EDWARD VI
(d.1553)

Arthur
(d.1502)
m. Catherine
of Aragon

Margaret's line

m. James IV
(Stuart)
(d.1513)

m.Archibald
Douglas,e. of
Angus
(d.1557)

James V
(d.1542)
m. Mary of
Guise
(d.1560)

Margaret
m. Mathew
Stuart. e. of
Lennox
(d.1571)

Mary Queen
of Scots
(d.1587)

Mary's line

m.Louis XII
of France
(d.1515)

m.Charles
Brandon,d.of
Suffolk
(d.1545)

Frances
m. Henry
Grey, m. of
Dorset
(d.1554)

Eleanor
m. Henry
Clifford, e. of
Cumberland
(d.1570)

Jane Grey
(d.1554)

Margaret
(d.1596)

Part One

THE
BACKGROUND

1 Henry's Inheritance

TOWN AND COUNTRYSIDE

The Britain of Henry VIII was not well known geographically. The foreigners who described it seemed almost wholly dependent either on classical sources such as Caesar and Strabo or on the Venerable Bede. Polydore Vergil, who wrote a history of England which first came into print in 1513, starts with a description of the physical features and natural resources of the country, which bears a strong resemblance to that in Bede's *Ecclesiastical History* of A.D. 731. Vergil was not following Bede, however, when he divided Britain into four parts, which are inhabited by Englishmen, Scotsmen, Welshmen and Cornishmen, 'which all differ emonge themselves, either in tongue, either in manners, or ells in lawes and ordinances'. He divided England in turn into four more parts—the area south of the Thames, the Midlands south of the Trent, the six counties towards Wales and the seven northern counties (**20**).

These divisions are important, for they indicate that the country cannot be treated as a unit. The four parts of Britain Vergil described were clearly provinces with differences as pronounced as those of Castile, Navarre and Aragon in the Iberian peninsula. The north of England also had the characteristics of a province. Not only were the wild dales of Northumberland and the valleys of West Riding highly remote, but there were local jurisdictions which were often outside royal control, such as the liberties of Durham and Hexham and the hundred baronies and manors of the Percy family. These areas had come to see their border defences against the Scots as their own responsibility and their feuds against the Scottish border reivers as personal vendettas, even though the king kept a substantial garrison at Berwick.

England was predominantly an agricultural country, as were all the parts of Britain. From the point of view of agricultural production, it can be divided into two broad areas by a line drawn from the

River Tees in the north to Dorset in the south. To the west of this line the lands were mainly grass-growing uplands, which concentrated on animal husbandry. This involved more than just the rearing of sheep, though wool was England's staple product. It also included cattle-rearing or fattening, dairying or horse breeding. In these upland areas, arable farming was subsidiary to the pasture and only produced enough cereals for the needs of the farmer and his cattle.

To the east of the line were the lowlands, where the farming was usually a mixture of arable and pasture. The lowland farmer could concentrate on corn or grass, depending on the needs of the market. There was a growing incentive for farmers to produce for the market, as population in country and town grew and the demand for wool increased. In the mixed-farming area, there was a great variety in farming practice, depending on the type of soil and the nature of the local market. Arable crops were often grown for town market, while a few cattle were kept to graze and manure the fallow land, as happened on the wolds and brecklands of East Anglia. Cattle fattening was part of the rural economy in many counties. Cattle were often brought from the uplands to be fed on arable crops sown for the purpose in Leicestershire or Hertfordshire, or on the rich marshland grasses of Lincolnshire.

The need for the farmers to produce more and to adapt to local markets, put pressure on the common field system of farming. In the uplands, this was not serious as there was ample pasture. The traditions of pastoral farming led to enclosure by agreement, and there was no great urge to increase the arable fields. The problem was mainly in the lowlands, where increases in the number of cattle or sheep led to overstocking of the common pastures and waste, which were only meant to feed the animals that pulled the ploughs and manured the crops. In these communities enclosure by agreement was often thwarted by determined freemen; certainly it was the areas of mixed and arable farming that remained unenclosed in the sixteenth century (**68**), (**38**).

Many medieval towns had declined in the fifteenth century due to the smaller population and the less active market in agricultural produce. Others, however, emerged as centres of the cloth trade and as sea ports for cloth exports. A Venetian reporter of 1500 wrote that 'there are scarcely any ports of importance in the kingdom excepting these two: Bristol, a seaport to the west, and

Boraco, otherwise York, which is on the borders of Scotland; besides London to the south'. The ports and towns were small by continental, especially Italian standards, and even London was described by John Major in 1521 as being only one-third the size of Paris (5).

The cloth trade was becoming dominated by London. Blackwell Hall in London was the national cloth market, London capital dominated the commerce of other ports and cloth was being brought to London even from the West Riding and East Anglia. Bristol was benefiting from a vigorous trade with Spain, Ireland and Iceland, and Southampton from the annual visits of the carracks from Genoa and Venice, but even they were beginning to lose ground to London.

John Major thought that there were three things that contributed to the wealth of London; the supreme courts of justice, the almost constant presence of the king and the great concurrence of merchants. To these might be added London's ideal situation for supplying England's chief markets for broadcloth in Flanders and the Rhine delta. The city gave an impression of wealth with its line of goldsmiths' shops in Cheapside, and foreigners were impressed by the large number of people who possessed silver plate in their houses. Cloth was clearly the basis of considerable national wealth that was becoming continually more concentrated in London (59).

SOCIAL STRUCTURE

The nobles had lost the social power they exercised during the Wars of the Roses. The laws against the keeping of retainers in livery and against the manipulation of justice in the law courts were now being enforced, and many famous families, like the Mowbrays and Mortimers, had died out before the sixteenth century began. There were new noble families from the fifteenth century, such as the Courtenays and the Staffords, who were closely watched and vulnerable. The arrogant Edward Stafford, for instance, was to be executed in 1521. In general, however, new creations from among the king's servants did keep up aristocratic numbers, and an appearance of aristocratic predominance was maintained.

The manorial system no longer functioned as a social cement. There were very few bondmen who owed service to a lord; in most cases, the demesne land of the manor had been leased out to tenants when agriculture became less profitable in the fifteenth century. The most active remaining institution of the medieval manor was the manorial court administered by the steward. Many farmers in the manor held their land under customary law by copyhold tenure. Whenever land changed hands, the ownership of the land had to be confirmed by the steward and a copy of the terms of ownership exchanged. The entry fine demanded on changing hands was almost invariably 'reasonable', even if the amount of the fine was not specified in the copy. It amounted to a maximum of three years customary rent and was usually either one or two. In the event of non-satisfaction in the manor court, the copyholder could always take out a writ of trespass in a common law court against his eviction.

The copyholder was therefore almost as secure in his tenure as the freeholder, and together they formed the yeomen class of farmer. The gentleman knight, who owned one or more manors, was in an even better position to benefit from the buoyant market for agricultural produce. Often he no longer farmed the demesne himself, but let out the land usually for long terms of forty or sixty years. In this case, rent incomes would have decreased in value with the rise in prices. If, on the other hand, he farmed himself and had an enclosed demesne, the chances of profit were enormous (**40**).

There was no social barrier between the landowner and the trader. The aristocracy was only too willing to marry the well dowered daughters and widows of the merchants, as is illustrated by the interest of the fifteenth-century Pastons of Norfolk in London heiresses. There was also a habit of long ancestry, that those who made their fortune in trade should invest their capital in land. This was such a general occurrence that William Caxton, who had lived most of his life in Flanders, where the great merchant families stayed in trade, was astonished by the absence of merchant dynasties in London. The close interrelationship of land and trade makes it very misleading to talk of the rise of a middle class with its nineteenth-century meaning of a town class of merchants, financiers and industrialists.

The case for an influential rising middle class in the sixteenth century has always rested on the conversion of the landed class to middle-class business methods by the arrival of merchant land-owners in the countryside. There is no evidence that the improve-ment in agricultural efficiency and the movement away from subsistence farming to the production of food and raw materials for the market depended on such a stimulus. It can be better explained by the breakdown of the manorial economy, the growth of trade and the gradual increase in population. The chance of shrewd land purchases or sly enclosures was open to all landowners with foresight and influence, and it seems clear that it was the monopoly of no one class. Ruin was probably easier for a nobleman, who had the temptation of extravagance and display, than for a middling landowner, but this is not to say that the one was declining and the other rising. Similarly, the early Tudors often employed as their ministers men of humble origins, like Wolsey or Cromwell, but they still employed noble advisers, if they were loyal and hard-working. The idea of a rising middle class in the sixteenth century has been rightly dismissed as a myth by Professor Hexter (**36**). It is a concept that has distorted the whole interpretation of the Reformation and of the development of New Monarchy.

THE CHURCH

The Church still dominated society and the lives of the people. It was extremely wealthy and owned about a third of all land. The parish church was the focal point of each village community, and the village priest, although often extremely ignorant, the most educated man that many people would meet.

Popular religion was dominated by conventional cults based on saints, relics and pilgrimages, and a good deal of fear of the pain and punishment of Purgatory, yet there was no lack of piety. About half the books printed in England were aids to piety, such as devotional books, sermons, or lives of saints. Churches were well cared for and the standard of church observance was high.

Although people were in general contact with the Church, there was still a considerable undercurrent of dissent. The followers of John Wycliffe, called the Lollards, had been greatly persecuted as heretics and an Act for the burning of heretics (1401) and an Act forbidding English Bible translations unless sanctioned by the bishops (1408), had helped to drive them underground. The traditions of Lollardry lived on, copies of the Lollard Vernacular Bible continued to circulate and at the beginning of the sixteenth century, the Lollard movement began to revive. It spread among types 'of whom few or none were learned, being simple labourers and

7

artificers', according to Foxe (**6**). There was a large group of over 300 Lollards, whom Bishop Longland of Lincoln dealt with in Buckinghamshire in 1521, and there were numbers in London.

The prevalence of heresy in England from the end of the fourteenth century onwards had the effect of hardening the attitude of the English bishops to new ideas and the vernacular Bible. Whereas twenty complete translations of the Bible were made in Germany between 1466 and 1522, there was no English translation between Wycliffe's version and Tyndale's in 1526. When Protestants began to circulate their views more freely after 1530, several Lollard writings were adapted to suit their need. As Foxe illustrated, there was a definite link between the Lollards and the Reformation (**28**).

Neither the upper clergy nor the lower clergy commanded respect. The bishops too often left their diocesan duties to suffragans and gave their time to royal administration, if they were not absentee foreigners. Pluralism was also rife both among bishops and the middle group of church officials, the deans and the archdeacons. It was the ignorance of the ordinary clergy that became a subject of great importance to reformers like John Colet. 'For there is the well of evils, that, the broad gate of holy orders opened, every man that offereth himself is all where admitted without pulling back. Thereof springeth and cometh out the people that are in the Church both of unlearned and evil priests.'

Resentment against the clergy was enhanced by their privileges at law through benefit of clergy, and by their power and jurisdiction in the Church courts. These grievances were given wide publicity, in London at least, through the Hunne case (1514). Richard Hunne was taken before the Bishop of London's court in 1512 for refusing to give up his dead infant's shroud to the rector as a mortuary and found guilty. Hunne brought a countercharge against his rector of praemunire, which was never decided. Meanwhile Hunne was arrested and imprisoned for possessing some heretical books, including a Lollard Bible, but in 1514, before his trial, he was found dead in his cell. Anticlericalism was aroused in London by the verdict of wilful murder brought against the Bishop's chancellor and two others, including the gaoler, by the burning of Hunne's body as a heretic by Bishop Fitzjames and by the Bishop's unwillingness to allow his officers to be brought to trial for murder.

The Hunne affair became mixed up with the controversy over benefit of clergy, not only because the Bishop's officers and servants were involved, but also because the 1512 parliament had removed benefit temporarily from those in minor orders who had committed certain types of robbery or murder. The ability of anyone with a tonsure or with a smattering of Latin to claim benefit was an obvious abuse, yet Pope Leo X had again decreed clerical immunity from lay trial in 1514. When the issue was reconsidered by the 1515 parliament, it split opinion within the Church. A disputation was arranged between Abbot Kidderminster, who put the Church's case, and Dr Standish, a friar and court preacher, who questioned the right of the Church to accept Leo's decree and by implication accused the clergy in Convocation of praemunire. The King intervened, claiming that kings of England never had any superior but God alone, but did not define his sovereignty over the Church courts. Henry was content to save Standish from the wrath of the Church, while the case against the Bishop's chancellor in Hunne's case and the whole issue of benefit of clergy were dropped.

The sovereignty of the crown over the Church had been settled in the king's favour in the fourteenth century by the statutes of provisors and praemunire, when the acceptance of papal nominees for Church posts in England and of papal edicts became dependent on the king's approval. With the weakness of the Papacy during the fifteenth and early sixteenth centuries, the kings had little reason to use these weapons against papal interference, but they remained for use should royal authority be questioned by the Church. Praemunire was also an important charge against Wolsey, because he had exercised his authority over the English Church by his papal title of legate *a latere*.

Papal authority was also being questioned as a result of the new emphasis on the Bible. William Tyndale was the first important English convert to Lutheranism. He fled abroad in 1524, but his New Testament, published on the continent in 1526, was widely circulated in England, and its preface petitioned people to depend on the Bible as the authority for the doctrine, institutions and ceremonies of the Church. In the 1520s, a group of scholars used to meet in the White Horse Inn at Cambridge, which became known as 'Little Germany', to discuss Lutheran ideas; and many of them, including Latimer and Ridley, were later to become Protestant leaders. There was a similar movement among humanists like Colet, Erasmus and More, who brought the techniques of literary criticism to bear on the Bible and pointed out the disparity between

The Background

New Testament Christianity and the practices of the contemporary Church. The greatest achievement was Erasmus's Greek Testament (1516), but the technique of criticism had been known since Colet delivered his Oxford sermons in 1496. Although their criticism of the Church was not appreciated by the bishops, they remained loyal Catholics and had no desire to break the unity of the Church.

There were, therefore, many criticisms of the clergy at the beginning of the century, but the main threat to the Church came from the emphasis on the authority of the Bible and the king. Both of these were direct challenges to the authority of the Pope.

2 Cardinal Wolsey

HIS SIGNIFICANCE

The domination of Cardinal Wolsey over the affairs of England was so complete until 1530 that it can be considered as a prelude to the formative period of Henry's reign. Henry VIII was nearly eighteen when his father died, but, as Cavendish says, 'the King was young and lusty, disposed all to mirth and pleasure and to follow his desire and appetite, nothing minding to travail in the busy affairs of this realm' (**1**). He was capable of ruling from the very beginning, but at no time did he like office work. Henry was always an important power, demanding the loyalty of his ministers, but he was prepared to allow considerable initiative to those whom he trusted. The King's trust in Wolsey was complete. John Skelton the poet, called him 'the kynges derling', and it was only very rarely that Henry found it necessary to question Wolsey's decisions. Giustiniani, the Venetian ambassador reported in 1519: 'This Cardinal is the person who rules both the King and the entire kingdom' [**doc. 6**].

Wolsey had a unique control over the realm for a subject. Henry Beaufort in the fifteenth century had held the same important offices of cardinal, chancellor and legate *a latere*, but he had not had the same opportunity for exercising his authority, nor was he the archbishop of York. From 1518 onwards Wolsey had control over both Church and state. It has often been said that it was the example of his supremacy, that encouraged Henry to seek supremacy for himself after Wolsey's death, but it is improbable that Henry needed any such lesson (**56**).

Wolsey was renowned for his grandeur. He maintained sumptuous palaces and a household fit for a king. He acted out his precedence everywhere in ostentatious processions, led by his two cross-bearers, his two pillar-bearers and his beautifully dressed retainers. His calculated insults led long-serving ministers like Warham and Fox to leave the court, while the nobility and gentry were annoyed by

11

his intolerable arrogance. Yet as his enemy Polydore Vergil conceded, 'Wolsey carried on all business at his own will, since no one was of more value to the King' (**20**).

Warham's longevity as archbishop of Canterbury was one of Wolsey's saddest disappointments, for it deprived him of technical primacy over the Church in England. He more than compensated for the limitation of his supremacy by his promotion as legate *a latere*. His authority as legate was gradually extended both in time and power; eventually he held it for life and had power to reform the secular clergy, the monks and the friars, to grant degrees and to appoint to ecclesiastical benefices. The declared purpose behind his demands was the desire to reform the Church, but in fact he achieved little. He dissolved a number of small monasteries, but their revenues were diverted to his school at Ipswich and his college at Oxford. His own personal example suggests that he was troubled little by the abuses of his time. He was a notorious pluralist, always holding another bishopric in addition to York, and he was abbot of the rich abbey of St Albans, though he had never been a monk. He had two illegitimate children, whom he provided for in the Church, and he never visited any of his cathedrals.

The effect of his rule over the Church was to weaken the morale of the bench of bishops. As legate, Wolsey had superseded their powers, conducting his own visitation of benefices and monasteries within their jurisdiction. He had 'in every diocese through this realme all manner of spiritual ministers, as commissaries, scribes, apparitors and all other necessary officers to furnish his courts; and presented by prevention whom he pleased unto all benefices throughout all this realme and dominions thereof' (Cavendish, **1**). He also kept bishoprics vacant and encouraged the appointment of foreigners as bishops, so that he could 'farm' them for his own profit. One effect of his government was to end, temporarily, the practice of burning heretics, as the trial of heretics was taken out of the hands of the diocesan consistories. In fact the prevalence of Lutheranism at Cardinal's College, Oxford, suggests that heresy spread easily during his rule. The lack of positive leadership towards either reform or uniformity did nothing to improve the morale of the Church of England. Indeed, the taste of direct papal government through a legate *a latere*, which Wolsey provided, was an experience that weakened the allegiance of many clergymen to the Pope, whom he represented.

GOVERNMENT

Henry VIII inherited from his father an administrative system which was controlled by the king from within the household. Henry VII had taken a direct interest, especially in financial administration, which his son did not share. Although Henry VII's system of government worked well, it depended so much on his personal supervision, that it could not survive his son's indifference to routine matters. Both the Yorkists and Henry VII had intentionally bypassed institutions that were capable of outside domination, such as the Exchequer and the Lancastrian Council. They had retreated into the household and given their orders either orally or by means of the signet seal, while the royal revenues were, where possible, administered through the King's Chamber (**10**).

Henry VII's methods were continued after his death, mainly by the same civil servants. Sir John Heron, Treasurer of the Chamber, remained in office from 1492 to 1521, for instance. From 1515 onwards, the routine work of government was supervised by Cardinal Wolsey as lord chancellor, and while he lived, there was little change in government methods. One early change was the abolition of the office of Surveyor of the King's Prerogative, but this, like the execution of Empson and Dudley in 1510, was an attempt to win early popularity by ending supposed extortion. Two general surveyors of land were appointed in 1511, whose powers were defined in an Act of 1515. Their task was to supervise royal accountants, but they were dependent on the exchequer as their court of law and their court of record. They were merely providing the driving energy in the household, which Henry VIII had no desire to provide himself (**11**).

The first half of Henry's reign saw no change in the character of the Council. It had two main functions. First there was the court of the Star Chamber that for a century before 1487 had sat at Westminster during term time for the enforcement of law and order. Sir Thomas Smith was right when he said that 'this court began long before but took great augmentation and authoritie' under Cardinal Wolsey. After Wolsey became lord chancellor in 1515, he began a vigorous execution of the laws against riot oppressors and maintenance. As Hall says, 'he punyshed also lordes, knyghtes and men of all sortes for ryottes, beryng and maintenance in their countries, that the pore men lyved quietly'. He also tried cases formerly heard in the Church courts like forgery, perjury, libel and slander. Wolsey extended the buildings called the Star Chamber in 1517 and was in fact its real creator [**doc. 5**]. The other part was the council attendant on the king, which later in Henry VIII's reign was to be given a formal existence as a Privy Council. Kings always like to be surrounded by councillors who could advise them. Such advice was given quite informally and no records were kept of what was said. The domination of Wolsey over affairs between 1515 and 1530 hindered the development of the Privy Council, because he both became the King's sole adviser and attracted councillors to himself. The King and the Cardinal were rarely together, so the King was often deprived of advice; the Eltham Ordinances (1526) were a recognition of this. They said that two councillors at least were to wait on the King each morning and afternoon (**98, 99, 100**).

Although Wolsey was lord chancellor, it was not from this office that his administrative power emanated. His power came from the trust placed in him by the King. He held the great seal as chancellor, but he issued his orders by private letter or through the privy seal, which for most of his rule was in the hands of bishops whom Wolsey could influence. His work in chancery was judicial. Chancery was the court of the king's conscience, which developed a branch of law called equity. Equity was really the chancellor's private sense of justice and in Wolsey's hands tended to develop along law lines. Wolsey's pre-eminence over the law courts was such that he was able to establish a Court of Requests as a branch of Star Chamber and to issue commissions to local and central bodies to hear private suits. The expansion of prerogative justice was a threat to the common law courts, but it was necessary to redress the legal balance in the interests of the poor.

The crucial changes in administration and government took place after 1530. The period of Wolsey's domination did not produce any major innovation except perhaps the subsidy tax, first collected in 1514. Successful exploitation of this tax depended on a cooperative relationship with parliament, which Wolsey never developed. He would have done without parliament altogether if it had not been for the financial necessity created by the French war (1522–24). As it was, all goodwill had been lost by his attempt to collect a forced loan before the parliament was called and trust was broken by his 'anticipation' of the parliamentary revenue in 1523 and a further forced loan, the notorious Amicable Loan of 1525 [**doc. 9**].

FOREIGN POLICY

Henry VII had, where possible, pursued a policy of non-involvement on the continent. He was willing to defend his shaky title to the throne by bringing pressure on foreign powers to give up support for Yorkist pretenders and by arranging marriages with continental families; he was also quick to realise the potential threat to England presented by the French acquisition of the kingdom of Brittany. He avoided, however, any commitment in Italy, even though King Ferdinand of Aragon inveigled him into the Holy Alliance of 1496.

In contrast, Henry VIII and Wolsey became deeply involved in continental affairs, and at times seemed to lose sight of England's basic interests. From an economic point of view, England was becoming almost wholly dependent on Antwerp as the market for her broadcloth. The industry of Flanders, which was part of Burgundy, was in turn largely geared to the finishing and dyeing of English cloth. In 1516 Burgundy and Spain were united under the rule of Charles I, who, in 1519, also became Holy Roman Emperor as Charles V. As England had been closely bound to Spain by the Treaty of Medina del Campo (1489) and by the subsequent marriage of both Arthur and Henry to Catherine of Aragon, there were strong reasons why Wolsey should base his foreign policy on the Spanish alliance, as had Henry VII.

France was the traditional enemy. All English kings since Edward III claimed the title King of France, Calais remained as the last vestige of England's empire in France, and the francophobia of the Hundred Years War was not dead. The treaty of 1502 between James IV of Scotland and Henry VII did not mark the end of the 'Aulde Alliance' between France and Scotland, which in fact, was in existence throughout Henry VIII's reign.

The shifts of alliance during the period of Wolsey's dominance were so frequent that historians have sought to find some pervading principle. If Wolsey had really believed in a European balance of power, he would have pursued the French alliance more vigorously after 1519. He may well have desired a balance of power in north Italy. Whereas there was no particular advantage to be gained by possessing north Italy, except perhaps for prestige and booty, kings were clearly worried by its domination by one power. To Charles V Milan became a vital link between the different parts of his empire after 1519, but it had no such importance to Wolsey in 1516, when he enlisted the aid of the Swiss and Emperor Maximilian to eject Francis I after his victory at Marignano. It may also have been partly concern for the balance in north Italy which led Wolsey to organise the League of Cognac to eject the imperialists from north Italy after the battle of Pavia in 1525.

Professor Pollard linked Wolsey's interest in Italy with his desire to serve the interests of the Papacy, saying that Wolsey's unique dependence on Rome as legate *a latere* bound England and bound himself to a papal foreign policy. Wolsey became legate in 1518 and was seeking ways of having his appointment as legate extended for life until 1524, when he was successful, but he had very little loyalty or respect for the Popes. In 1517, he completely ignored Leo X's demand for a crusade and used the visit of Campeggio, the papal legate in 1518, both as a bargaining counter for his own position as legate and as a platform for his own treaty of perpetual peace (1518). Henry's attitude to the Papacy was identical, as he too had a desire for an additional royal title, which he was granted in 1521, and was extremely keen that Wolsey's candidature for the Papacy should succeed. Wolsey was no more and no less a servant of the Papacy than Henry himself.

J. J. Scarisbrick has concentrated on the eight years of peace from 1514 to 1522 as the most characteristic period of Wolsey's diplomacy (**62**). Wolsey's main desire was for peace, and his greatest triumph was the Treaty of London (1518), which bound the twenty powers that signed it to perpetual peace. During these years he achieved the treaties of 1514 and 1518 and the meeting with France on the Field of the Cloth of Gold. He also met Charles V at Sandwich and Gravelines in 1520, and signed the Treaty of Bruges with him in 1521. The Venetian ambassador was probably right when he said of Wolsey: 'Nothing pleases him more than to be called the arbiter of the affairs of Christendom.'

Wolsey wanted positive involvement in the continent, but it was Henry who demanded the wars. Henry had sworn to make war on France immediately after his accession, and favoured the wars against France in 1512 and 1522 and the intervention in north Italy in 1516. Wolsey made his reputation as the organiser of the expedition to north France in 1513 and took full responsibility for the other wars because he was always the King's loyal servant, but they were not necessarily his wars.

Professor Wernham sees the secret treaty of aggression that Henry made with Charles V in 1521 as part of a plan to guarantee the future of the Tudor dynasty in England. The main ingredient of the treaty was not the plan to conquer and partition France, but the promise that Charles V would marry Princess Mary, Henry's daughter, when she reached the age of twelve in 1528. The prospect of a daughter inheriting the throne worried Henry and he wanted her married to someone who could assure her peaceful succession. The only queen England had had in the past was Queen Matilda and her reign had led to nineteen years of civil war, so the precedent suggested the need for positive action. Henry hoped for the fulfilment of his concept of 'the whole monarchy of Christendom' under the Emperor in 1525 after Charles had crushed the French at Pavia. His hopes were quickly shattered when there was no partition of France and when Charles V married the twenty-two-year-old Isabella of Portugal (**70**).

In 1526 Wolsey encouraged, but did not join, the League of Cognac against the victorious Charles V. He wanted to act as arbiter between the two sides. Even the treaty with France made at Westminster in April 1527 was only to become active if Charles V refused to treat. Had Wolsey's main motives been concern for the interests of the Papacy, or for the balance of power, he would have acted with rather more urgency than this, though finance by this time had become a very real problem. Wolsey had a desire to be an arbiter and peace-maker, but these aims were incompatible with the belligerence of Henry and the faithlessness of the continental kings.

Part Two

DESCRIPTIVE
ANALYSIS

3 Administration

ADMINISTRATIVE CHANGE

There had to be administrative changes in Henry's reign to cope with the new sources of revenue. New institutions were needed, for instance, to administer the income of the Church and the monastic lands which came under royal control. As the national policies became more grandiose and controversial, it was also necessary for the King to improve the return from his sources of finance and to refine his control over the outer parts of his realm in the North and Wales. The extension and improvement of royal control over the kingdom had been progressing since 1471, but was completed in Henry VIII's reign, in the sense that the institutions by which England was governed until the Civil War were given their characteristic shape under Henry VIII. The most important of these was the Privy Council, as the nerve centre of Tudor government with the subsidiary regional councils in the North and Wales. All of these were formalised during the period of Cromwell's dominance from 1530 to 1540 and owe much to his vision and energy. These councils, together with the Court of Star Chamber and the Court of Requests, provided a series of courts exclusively under royal control, through which England could be governed and order maintained.

These administrative changes form the basis of the conciliar government of the Tudors, but it is in the agencies of finance and the government departments that Dr Elton has discerned an administrative revolution (**34**). The revolution was the change from administration through the household on an informal basis, where the success of government depended on the personality of the king, to government through bureaucratic departments which had a procedure and staff laid down by statute, so that business was transacted despite changes of minister or king. The regulation of departments in this way had occurred earlier in the reign when the functions of the general surveyors were defined by statute and the Exchequer had been a bureaucratic department outside the household since the twelfth century, but the formalisation of all government departments, including the household itself, can be shown to have been hurried along by Thomas Cromwell. Apart from refinements and reforms, the Tudor system of departments under royal control, but outside the household, was not irrevocably replaced until the nineteenth century, when ministers became responsible to parliament and civil servant appointments were opened to public competition.

Whether the development of bureaucracy can be attributed solely to Cromwell is open to doubt. The reform of most of the financial departments occurred after his death and could be interpreted as an attempt by routine bureaucrats, upset by Cromwell's highly personal methods of administration, to bring back order and method into the system of finance. An objection to the idea that Cromwell replaced 'government by king' by 'government under a king' through the establishment of the Privy Council, is the way in which the Privy Council failed to keep order and remain united during the minority after Henry's death (**101**). It showed itself to be still capable of being little more than a disparate body of magnates, ecclesiastics and officials. Many of Cromwell's methods were so personal, that it is better to see him as a reforming minister during a time of change rather than as a revolutionary minister.

AGENCIES OF FINANCE

The Chamber had been developing as an institution since the Wars of the Roses. It was a department within the household which was completely under royal control and was far more open to royal direction than the Exchequer. It was used in particular by the Yorkists and Henry VII for the more profitable management of the king's private landed estates, but other sources of revenue were transferred to it, so that in Henry VII's reign it controlled considerably more of the total revenues of England than the Exchequer (**30**). The Chamber never in any sense replaced the Exchequer, which continued to control the accounts of the sheriffs (the pipe rolls), escheators, and the customs men. It was, however, the key office in the painstaking exploitation of profits from wards, liveries, butlerage, woods, the king's mines and vacant bishoprics and abbacies. The clerk of the pipe, the "engrosser of the great roll of the Exchequer", complained in 1529 that the profits of his office were greatly diminished because all the "great accountants" were declaring their accounts before the general surveyors instead of accounting at the Exchequer. The key officers in the Chamber were the two general surveyors appointed in 1511. They were the former chief officials of Henry VII's court of audit with responsibility for the accuracy of other revenue officers as well.

After 1530 there was a decline in the income from most sources, at a time when there was a growing demand for money, particularly for defence. This was a source of anxiety to Sir Brian Tuke, Treasurer of the Chamber 1528–45, an unimaginative but not an incompetent man, who complained of the lack of supervision from the king and the failure of the general surveyors to make a monthly audit. The king and court were keeping money in the king's privy purse and spending it without warrant. Such an haphazard system had driven Tuke "almost totally in to extreme dispaire". The Chamber was being deprived of revenue not only for these reasons, but also because new financial courts were founded to administer the new sources of royal income from the Church and the monasteries.

The Act of 1534 laying down the administrative details concerning the collection of first fruits and tenths intended that existing machinery should be used and that the money should be paid into the Chamber, but it developed very differently under Cromwell's direction. John Gostwick, who became the treasurer of first fruits and tenths in 1535, previously administered sources of income which Cromwell had cornered for his own projects, which came to include first fruits and tenths. Cromwell's manipulation of finance during his first years as a minister gave no indication of his later orderly intentions. He used his minor offices as Keeper of the Jewels, Clerk of the Hanaper, and Chancellor of the Exchequer, all of which he held for life, to build up a spending department under his own control in the jewel house (**34**).

Although Cromwell had his own personal treasury within the household, which he administered in an informal way without a proper department, it was clear that he preferred departments of state for the administration of finance. By 1542 six financial departments had been developed. Two of these were financial departments, which remained unchanged, as they were departments of state already. These were the Exchequer Court and the Court of the

Duchy of Lancaster. Fundamental reform began with the establishment of the Court of Augmentations by statute in 1536. It was a court of record and had 'one great seal and one privy seal'; its whole membership, function and authority were defined in the statute. Its first chancellor was Richard Rich, but it was dominated by Cromwell, the Vicar General. The establishment of three other departments of state between 1540 and 1542 became the more necessary, once Cromwell's personal energy and supervision had been removed. A Court of First Fruits and Tenths was established in 1540, a Court of Wards in 1540, which was adapted into a Court of Wards and Liveries in 1542, and a Court of General Surveyors in 1542. Each court was independent in itself, capable of establishing itself as a tribunal in its own cases and had its own system of revenue collection and audit.

The new revenue courts were kept fairly well drained of funds, especially during the war with France from 1542 to 1546. During this time, the Mint became "our holy anchor" as the king realised the ease with which profit could be made by debasing the coinage. The Mint was especially reorganised for the purpose and yielded a profit of £363,000 between May 1544 and January 1547, which was only marginally less than the receipts of the Court of Augmentations during the same period. Just before the end of the reign, an effort was made to improve the revenues of crown lands by introducing a more centralised system of audit. Lands and possessions under the survey of the Court of General Surveyors and the Court of Augmentations were apportioned by counties to twelve new auditors, who drew up a single account of the gross value of the revenues of each county (**60**).

This process of amalgamation was continued after Henry's death. The multiplication of the systems of rent collection and audit was obviously wasteful and there was a need for more centralisation of finance. This was achieved in 1554 by the dissolution of the Court of Augmentations, which since 1547 had also incorporated the Court of General Surveyors, and the Court of First Fruits and Tenths. The reason given in Mary's letters patent dissolving the Court of Augmentations was that the monastic property entrusted to the Court had been 'as well by gifts and grants of our said late father as our said dear brother, dispersed, cut away and greatly dismembered'.

The result was that control of finance returned to the Lord

Treasurer in the Exchequer, although for administrative reasons the Court of Wards and of the Duchy of Lancaster were retained. The Chamber was virtually unused as a treasury towards the end of Henry's reign and after his death became once again just a household department. The introduction of bureaucratic finance during the reign had been mainly an expedient to cope with new sources of finance, but once revenues departments were formed and re-organised, there was no room for the informal methods of the Chamber.

THE SECRETARY

Thomas Cromwell's pre-eminence in the king's favour from 1531 to 1540 enabled him to become a directing force in every aspect of government policy. He had oversight of foreign diplomats, he arranged the religious changes, he had responsibilities in defence, he supervised the household and had his own personal financial treasury. During this period he held three offices of an administrative nature; he was the king's principal secretary from 1534 to 1540, Master of the Rolls from 1534 to 1536 and Lord Privy Seal from 1536 to 1540. Of these, it was the secretary's office that was elevated in importance. By 1540 it had become a department of state outside the household and the secretary was named among the great officers of state. This rise in status for the office was not just a reflection of Cromwell's importance, for he already held a higher position in the order of precedence as the king's Vicar General and Lord Privy Seal.

After the resignation of Sir Thomas More as Lord Chancellor in 1532, Cromwell was expected by his contemporaries to take this office. The Lord Chancellor had a long-established seniority in the administration as the keeper of the Great Seal. It was the office that Wolsey had held, and it may have been the ceremonial exposure of the office that Cromwell disliked. The linking factor in the offices that he did accept was that they all had a secretariat. The Secretary controlled the signet seal, the Lord Privy Seal had his own seal and the Mastership of the Rolls had responsibility for part of the Chancery secretariat, which in turn had access to the Great Seal. Cromwell's motive, as in his accumulation of an odd collection of financial offices, was that he wished to keep a close watch on the instruments for carrying out orders. The use

25

which he made of his hold over the seals does not suggest a very tidy or systematic mind, merely one that felt insecure without control.

If the Act of 1536 'concerning the clerkes of the signet and privie seal' is taken alone, it does suggest that Cromwell was trying to impose the dead hand of bureacratic routine upon the use of the seals. The Act said that no warrant, even if it was signed by the king, was to be sealed with the great seal unless a warrant had previously been obtained from the principal secretary or clerk of the signet and also the keeper of the privy seal. Similarly, orders under the privy seal were first to be authenticated by the signet. Such a channel for warrants had been ordered in 1444 without effect and this act was also ineffective because Cromwell did not observe it himself. It may have been true that Cromwell wanted bureaucratic organisation for the new state but not for himself, or it may have been that Cromwell was not so interested in the controls after he became Lord Privy Seal himself in 1536.

Seals ceased to play an originating part in the routine business of government. The use of the privy seal declined as the new financial agencies began to possess and use their own seals, but the signet did not take over the function of originating all government action as was envisaged in the 1536 Act. The developing part of the secretary's office was not the signet clerks' department but the secretary's personal staff. They enforced orders which carried Cromwell's signature and they seem originally to have been trained in his private household. In fact, Cromwell channelled orders through this part of the secretary's office, which previously would have been handled by the privy seal.

The privy seal and the signet did not lose all their importance; the privy seal, for instance, remained the seal of the conciliar courts. They ceased, however, to be the vital originators of government action. Cromwell made great use of the state paper, that is an order bearing his signature, issued by his secretary's office, which could now be called a department of state (**34**).

The secretary's office itself did not hold its position after Cromwell's fall in 1540. Its division into two parts in 1540 was not so much a recognition that the work of the office had grown as a scheme to provide the king with a secretary attendant at the court as well as one attached to the Council at Westminster. Although there were not always two secretaries after this, it eventually became the norm in the seventeenth century. It was in Elizabeth's reign that the principal secretaries became the chief governing ministers in home and foreign affairs. This was the fulfilment of Cromwell's design for the secretary's office, not a routine department in the image of the 1536 Act, but a department of state.

THE COUNCIL

There were very many people who called themselves councillors in Henry VIII's reign, as there had been in his father's time. The first known list of his reign dates from 1520, when forty-one peers and bishops are named as well as 'all knights and others of the king's council'. Many of these would give service and advice in peripheral councils such as 'his counsel learned in the law' and 'his spiritual counsel', which were of little importance, or his provincial councils in Calais or the North. It is the minority of the council, who were attendant on the king or holding court in the Star Chamber and at Whitehall, that form the effective council.

During the period of Wolsey's domination, the judicial aspects of the Council had been developed to the detriment of its political and administrative functions. Little distinction had been made during Henry VII's reign between the councillors who gave advice and those who administered justice (**43**). Councillors meeting in Star Chamber could be fulfilling either function, as there were two chambers in the building, one of them suitable for a council attending the king, the other for the council sitting as a court. There was also no difference in composition or function between the councillors attending the king wherever he was and the council in the Star Chamber at Westminster. They remained one Council. In Wolsey's hands, however, the judicial work was increased, while he alone gave the King advice (**98, 99**).

The great change that occurred after Wolsey's fall was the differentiation of the two functions of the Council, so that in 1540 the Privy Council was given a formal existence of its own, with its own clerk and its own register of proceedings and became clearly separated from the Court of Star Chamber. There was continuity with the past, as the senior clerk of the Council was attached to the Star Chamber and the junior clerk to the Privy Council. It was this division of staff that gave the Star Chamber technical superiority and the right to claim direct descendance from the medieval

King's Council, but it was the Privy Council that became the nerve centre of Tudor government (**100**).

In 1540 the Privy Council had nineteen members, most of them leading officers of state and household, some of whom were always attendant on the king. Some of the King's Council had always been *coram rege et consilio suo ubicunque fuerit*, but there was no sign of formal membership and procedure until after Wolsey's death. The reforms of the Council envisaged in the Eltham Ordinance, which was drawn up by Wolsey in 1526, stated that twenty 'honourable, virtuous, sad, wise, expert and discreet persons of the Council' were to attend the king, but they were to deal with both judicial and administrative matters and therefore were to incorporate the Star Chamber's functions. There was also to be a smaller council of nine giving continual attendance on the king. The ordinance was never enforced, but there is a close resemblance between the council named in the ordinance and the later Privy Council as far as membership is concerned.

When Henry devoted himself to government in his middle years, he was far more concerned with high politics than with law and order and these matters were better treated in a privy council than in the public court of Star Chamber. In the absence of evidence it was usually assumed that it emerged gradually into use again after 1530 before being formalised in 1540. Such evidence as there is, however, suggests that there was a privy council permanently in attendance on the king after 1536 with very similar membership to the Privy Council of 1540. Thomas Derby, the holder of the junior clerkship of the council was described in 1533 as 'clarke of our counsaill attending uppon our person' and as 'clerk of the privy council' in 1538. It is consistent with the rest of Cromwell's work that he should have produced an institutionalised privy council out of the council attendant sometime between 1534 and 1536. While he lived Cromwell was very much chief of the Council; he handled its clerical work through his own secretarial organisation. It was his fall that made the formalisation of the Privy Council necessary in 1540 (**34**).

Although it is possible to distinguish the Privy Council from the Star Chamber after 1540, they were still served by the same people. The Star Chamber, in addition, had the services of the chief justices of the King's Bench and the Common Pleas and at times recruited from among 'the councillors at large' or any peers or bishops that the Chancellor chose to summon. It met twice a week in term time, it was extremely popular and came to specialise in information of riots and tampering with juries. As far as Sir Thomas Smith was concerned in his book *De Republica Anglorum* (1583), its main function was to deal with riot. 'For that is the effect of this court, to bridle such noblemen or gentlemen which would offer wrong by force to any manner man and cannot be content to demand or defend the right by law and order.'

Another important part of the Council's jurisdiction was administered through the Court of Requests. An important function of the Council was to receive petitions and redress grievances and during Richard III's reign, perhaps earlier, certain councillors were deputed to be a regular tribunal for poor men's causes. The task of this committee of Council was to attend to the petitions put forward by those too poor to sue at common law. In 1516 Wolsey appointed councillors to sit in the White Hall of the Palace of Westminster 'for the expedition of poor men's causes depending in the Star Chamber', and by 1529 this court had grown into an established Court of Requests. The Court was at its height during Henry's reign and people other than poor men and king's servants were bringing their cases. It administered a species of equity like that of chancery, though there was always a common lawyer in the court during Henry's reign to make sure that land settlements conformed to the common law. It lacked the prestige of Star Chamber and was therefore later vulnerable to common law attacks.

THE NORTH AND WALES

The king's control of the North and of Wales and the Marches remained very imperfect, despite the councils that had been attached to the households of trustworthy noblemen in those areas by the Yorkists and Henry VII. These were temporarily revived by Wolsey in 1525 and 1526, when he delegated to Lady Mary's Council for Wales and the Duke of Richmond's Council for northern parts the hearing of all Star Chamber cases arising in their areas. For a time, Richmond's jurisdiction extended to the whole of England north of the Trent except for Durham. This was a return to the earlier expedient of using members of the royal family to rule Wales and the North.

These schemes were merely attempts at decentralisation, but

under Cromwell there was a determined attempt to incorporate the northern area into the central state system. The main problem here was to extend the jurisdiction of the king's writ to every corner of the kingdom. Rights of manorial jurisdiction made little difference as copyholders and freemen felt able to use the king's court (**40**). There were, however, a number of liberties, which either technically or in fact, were not under the king's law. The most blatant example was the Palatinate of Durham, which was an ecclesiastical liberty retaining a palatine organisation over which the King had little control. The Palatinate of Lancaster was also a separate jurisdiction, but since 1399 it had belonged to the crown. Other liberties, like Ripon, could keep out the king's sheriff and thus provided a safe sanctuary from the king's writ. An Act of 1536 abolished these liberties, making them subject to the normal royal justice administered by J.P.s and circuit judges. There were some exceptions which continued to differentiate Durham and Lancaster, especially the franchise enjoyed by the bishop of Durham and the archbishop of York to act as J.P.s (which was soon withdrawn) (**37**).

Two statutes of 1536 and 1543 organised the remaining part of Wales into shires, brought them under English law and introduced administration based on J.P.s. The incorporation of Wales into the English state was a great triumph, made possible by the energy of Rowland Lee as president of the Council of the Marches and also by the close connection of the Tudors with Wales.

Cromwell was also responsible for reorganising the provincial councils in these areas. The Council of the North had never effectively controlled the whole of the North before 1537 and even though the new Council's commission extended to all the North except the Duchy of Lancaster, it soon had to concede control of the Border Marches to the wardens of the East, Middle and West Marches. The importance of the new council of 1537 was that it was no longer attached to a nobleman's household, but was a separate bureaucratic council with a fixed membership. It was in no sense a branch of the Council; it exercised its jurisdiction in civil and criminal matters on the basis of its own commissions of the peace and of oyer and terminer. It was, however, closely supervised by the Privy Council in both judicial and administrative matters. It no longer had any responsibility for administering royal estates, which had been a function of the former noblemen's councils (**75**).

The Council of Wales and the Marches had a parallel history, but whereas the Council of the North seemed to be a strengthening of government after the Pilgrimage of Grace (1536), the Council of Wales was formed so that 'the king's loyal subjects may be relieved from the necessity of repairing to the council or the king's courts at Westminster'. It had, therefore, more of the character of a branch of the Council, though in other ways it was similar to the Council of the North. Its authority was extended all over Wales and the border shires mainly by the energy of Rowland Lee, who was president from 1534 to 1543. Although it had similar legal authority to the Council of the North, its jurisdiction was somewhat diminished by the establishment of four Courts of Great Sessions under permanent judges who were to hold assizes twice a year in each of the twelve Welsh shires.

A third council, the Council of the West, had a short existence after the Courtenays were suspected of plotting with Reginald Pole in 1538, but its authority was soon disregarded. The councils in the provinces did not solve any of the problems of distance, but they do indicate Cromwell's intention on the king's behalf to bring the whole realm under royal government.

LOCAL GOVERNMENT

The early Tudors had nothing to fear from baronial or manorial courts as rivals to their own courts in the localities. The manor courts still existed but they were mainly concerned with manorial administration. Nor was there any insuperable challenge to their authority from overmighty subjects. There was no necessity for them to keep a standing army nor did the nobility possess any privileges outside the common law. Sheriffs had ceased to be used except for routine purposes such as executing writs or supervising elections and were only appointed for a year, because they had been open to noble influence in tampering with the King's justice.

The countryside was ruled, therefore, by the chief people of the locality, who came to accept local government as part of their function and as a confirmation of their social status. They were commissioned to fulfil some task by the king and the most common of these was the commission of the peace. The justices of the peace were appointed for a year at a time, but received no pay except for four shillings a day allowed to them during Quarter Sessions under a statute of Richard II. The office of justice of the peace already had a long history, but it was during the sixteenth century that its importance and work increased. By 1547, according to Lambarde, there were 193 statutes that the justices were expected to enforce. Some were enforceable by one justice, some by a small group, which is the origin of petty sessions, but the J.P.s were at their most powerful at Quarter Sessions. Only at Quarter Sessions did they have juries to represent the county in the presentation and indictment of prisoners. It was ensured that some of the justices were lawyers. Further guarantees of fair trial were added in 1542 and 1543 when the justices of assize were given power to hear charges of negligence and abuse against J.P.s and to demand a transcript of proceedings (**37**).

As new statutes added to the supervisory work of justices, their function in administration began to increase. As a guarantee that the work was being done, a statute of 1542 tried to add more formal sessions to be held six weeks before Quarter Sessions, at which the enforcement of certain Acts concerning such things as vagabonds, archery and unlawful games could be enforced. It was also hoped that the justices would divide themselves up so that there were two to each hundred. It proved impossible to make the justices work in such a systematic way and in 1545, the scheme was abandoned. In the same year, recognition was given to the justice, called the *custos rotulorum*, who kept the rolls of the peace, when it was enacted that he should be appointed by the crown. The practice of keeping records helped to regularise the Quarter Sessions as a court.

A new official was appointed by Henry VIII to take responsibility for levying and mustering the militia. The commission of array was a medieval means of raising the shire levies and Henry continued the expedient of laying the burden of expense on the counties. During the Pilgrimage of Grace he placed the Duke of Suffolk, the Earl of Shrewsbury and the Earl of Derby in command of the armies raised in certain shires and gave them the title of king's lieutenants. Similar commissions were issued in 1545 to organise the defence of the south. These appointments were the predecessors of the lords lieutenant, who were usually privy councillors and most influential men in their counties, who took over responsibility for the county musters from the sheriffs on a permanent basis after 1585. They are another example of the way that the most powerful men in the county were employed in the service of the state (**63**).

4 Parliament

The concept of two Houses of Parliament was very new in the sixteenth century. The House of Lords was descended from the king's *magnum concilium* and it was referred to as the Parliament Chamber. No instance of its being called the House of Lords has been found before 1544. Originally it was the Parliament proper, but in the course of the sixteenth century, and probably by the end of Henry VIII's reign, it became just one of two Houses of Parliament. The Commons originated as a committee of Parliament. They attended the opening and closing ceremonies, but otherwise they met elsewhere, usually in the chapter-house of Westminster Abbey to fulfil the tasks that the king had assigned to them. During the fourteenth and fifteenth centuries, the deliberations of the Commons grew in importance. In addition to their traditional function of approving taxation, they had become an important court for the consideration of public bills. These bills became statutes if approved by Crown, Lords and Commons and had long been regarded as the highest expression of law in the realm (**55**). The legal sovereignty of statute made by king in Parliament was assured by the use that was made of it to complete the breach with Rome during the Reformation Parliament 1529–36.

THE LORDS

During Henry VIII's reign there was a real partnership of interests between the King and Parliament against the Church. The presence of bishops and abbots in the House of Lords did not detract from this as so many of them were appointed by the king and were attracted to royal service. The temporal lords were in no sense a caste. Their capacity to challenge the throne had been severely curtailed by the demise of many noble families during the fifteenth century and by the severe repression of the Yorkists and any others who suggested, like Edward Stafford, Duke of Buckingham in

1523, that they were fit to be king. Parliament was a court, capable of bringing subjects to trial, but this weapon was used during Henry's reign only for bringing the king's enemies to trial by bill of attainder. The weapon of impeachment, by which the king's ministers could be tried and convicted in the House of Lords, was not used during the whole Tudor period. There was also no social division between Lords and Commons. The baron was little different from the knight of the shire in social standing and wealth and originally both would have been called barons. The eldest son inherited the barony and sat in the Lords, while his brothers could sit in the House of Commons. In these circumstances there was unlikely to be any friction of interests between these two sections of both Houses.

A picture of the opening of the 1523 Parliament in the Royal Library, Windsor, gives a clear idea of the appearance of the House of Lords. The royal throne stood at one end, where the king sat surrounded by his leading councillors. In the middle of the room, four woolsacks were arranged in a square (only one of which now survives) on which sat the judges. The two clerks also rested on one of them to make the record, kneeling on the floor to do so. Outside this inner square sat the bishops and abbots on the right of the king and the peers on the left, while the Commons led by their Speaker stood behind the bar facing the king. This arrangement reflected the fact that the king's permanent Council was originally the core of the Parliament. An Act of 1539 tried to perpetuate the tradition by which leading officers of the crown and great household officials, whether noblemen or not, attended, but apart from the Lord Chancellor, none of them did attend, unless they were peers. The judges remained as observers, but took no part in the proceeding unless they were consulted.

Until the dissolution of the monasteries there was a fairly even balance between lords spiritual and lords temporal. During the course of the Reformation Parliament 1529–36, there were 50 lords spiritual, made up of 21 archbishops, bishops and custodians of spiritualities (who could represent the diocese) and 29 abbots, and 57 lords temporal, made up of 3 dukes, 2 marquises, 13 earls, 1 viscount and 38 barons (**42**). They always met as a single house and decisions were taken by majority vote regardless of estate. This could have been important had the Church been united in its opposition to the Reformation, but there was no such demonstration of solidarity until the Act of Uniformity 1559. Anyway there were various methods by which the king could control the lords. Potential opponents were summoned to attend, but it was made clear to them that they should stay away. Lords who could not attend could name a proctor to vote for them by proxy. In 1534 the abbots of Hyde and Hulme, both supporters of the government, held six and seven proxies respectively, and often Thomas Cromwell was given blank proxies to dispose of as he thought fit. These proctorial votes therefore gave the government a built-in advantage in the House of Lords, but there is no evidence that the government manipulated this convention unscrupulously (**95**). The fact remains that opposition from the House of Lords was fairly rare.

THE COMMONS

In 1529 there were 310 members of the Commons: 74 knights of the shire, elected from 37 counties, and 236 burgesses representing 117 parliamentary boroughs. All the boroughs were double-member constituencies, except for London, which returned 4 members. Relatively few new seats were created during Henry's reign, when it is considered that most of the new seats (31 out of 45) arose from the shiring of Wales, Monmouth and Cheshire in 1536 (**42**).

There was still quite a strong social difference between the county representatives and the borough members at this time, a difference that was to have disappeared by the end of the century. The county members, the knights of the shire, were elected by the forty-shilling freeholders, a franchise established by statute in 1430. Two of them sat for most counties and they were usually chosen from among the courtiers and local magnates. As in the boroughs, elections were rarely necessary, as certain families were accepted as being preeminent. In the boroughs, there were statutes of the fifteenth century which imposed residential qualifications on borough representatives, and these seem to have been observed. The invasion of the borough seats by the country gentlemen had hardly begun and burgesses were returned in large numbers. It has been estimated that there were two burgesses for every country gentleman sitting for borough seats in the Reformation Parliament. The franchise in the boroughs depended on the wording of the royal charter, which allowed them to be represented in the House of Commons, but in practice, although they varied greatly, most elections seem to have been controlled by the municipal corporations. In some of these boroughs, the payment of two shillings a day to members was such a burden that they were glad to give their seat to a country gentleman who would serve without pay. The House of Commons, however, had not yet achieved the social homogeneity which was so noticeable by the reign of Elizabeth.

There was something to attract the potential member to the Commons in the proximity of the king's court and courts of law in Westminster. There was also the possibility of presenting private bills (**96**). These were often to the benefit of particular towns, such as acts of 1534 which allowed Norwich and King's Lynn to take over properties that remained derelict, or to individuals. The private bills benefiting individuals often confirmed either the king or influential magnates in possession of their land. In addition, private members were allowed more participation in the drafting of public bills in committees, that were held before the bill was submitted to the floor of the House. These were different from modern parliamentary committees, which are appointed to discuss and amend bills already before the House, but this type of committee also met on occasions. There was, therefore, a growing capacity for members to participate in government, but there was no sign yet of a devouring enthusiasm for the task. During the third session of the Reformation Parliament 1532, when they were considering very important anticlerical matters concerned with the Supplication against the Ordinaries, the Commons begged to be allowed home. The Speaker, Thomas Audley, 'beseched the King to consider what payne, charge and cost his humble subjectes of the Nether House had susteyned syth the begynnynge of this Parliamant'. For many, attendance at Parliament was still an irksome task.

THE TRIUMPH OF STATUTE

The use of statute to complete the break with Rome extended its competence to virtually everything. Statute was made by King, Lords and Commons and to all intents and purposes it became sovereign. The breach with Rome was carried into effect by statute. The Pope's right to tax the English Church was abolished by the Act of Annates and the Dispensations Act abolishing Peter's Pence in 1534 and his power to exercise jurisdiction over English church courts was stopped by the Act in Restraint of Appeals 1533. Finally, the fact of the king's supremacy over the Church was declared by statute in 1534. The king's supremacy over church doctrine was enforced by statute in 1539 and 1543 and even if the doctrine was sometimes debated and agreed by the king's archbishops, bishops and other learned clergy outside Parliament, Parliament was here legislating on matters that before 1533 would have been outside its jurisdiction.

The extensive use which was made of statute during this time coincides with Cromwell's rise to power and there is no reason to doubt that Cromwell advised Henry to use Parliament in this way. It was he who resurrected the Supplication against the Ordinaries as the prelude to a campaign against the church courts in 1532, using a weapon first contemplated by the Commons in 1529 but never properly used. This manoeuvre succeeded in bringing the Church's legal independence to the king's notice and in forcing the eventual surrender by the clergy of their right to make canons except under royal licence. It was he also who drafted and recommended the Act of Restraint of Appeals in 1533. This was the occasion when Cromwell was described by Chapuys as 'powerful with the king'. Cromwell had a very extreme interpretation of statute. He must have read Marsiglio of Padua's book *Defensor Pacis*, which was written in 1324, but only published in an English edition in 1535, probably with Cromwell's help. Marsiglio not only believed that the sovereign should rule both Church and State, but also believed that no other laws should limit the sovereignty of the positive law (statute). Such ideas of the sovereign state, unfettered by tradition or outside jurisdiction were very new and few people other than Cromwell would have grasped their real significance [**doc. 14**].

The more common approach was that there were practical limitations to the power of statute. The medieval view was that statutes did not make law, but merely declared it as an interpretation of the natural law and this notion lingered on. Natural law was the reflection of the eternal law in man's nature and was therefore as perfect a realisation of God's law as was possible for man. The idea that statute law was limited by the natural law or the divine law was widely held both before and after the Reformation. Fortescue before and Hooker afterwards held to this view. Christopher St German, the most articulate legal thinker in Henry VIII's reign wrote that 'the law of man, the which sometimes is called the law positive, is derived by reason as a thing which is necessarily and probably following the law of reason and of the law of God'. It became very important when judges had to interpret statute law in the courts, as it provided a set of absolute standards that could be applied.

A less widely held view was that statute was limited by the law of God. This was mainly a justification for opposition to Reformation statutes as in the case of Thomas More, who refused the oath to accept the succession in 1534 because it was based 'upon an act directly repugnant to the laws of God and His Holy Church'. The Dispensations Act 1534, which transferred the power of dispensation to the Archbishop of Canterbury, declared that the power did not stretch to Holy Scripture and the law of God. As a theoretical limitation to statute, however, neither the law of God nor the law of nature was effective because the king in Parliament became the ultimate arbiter of what constituted the law in these cases, once royal supremacy over the Church was established [**doc. 23**].

The practical limitation to statute arose from the necessity for judges to interpret the law when they applied it. During the fifteenth century, judges had distinguished between statutes which made new law and statutes which declared existing law. The first were interpreted to the letter, the second were open to equitable construction by the judges. During the Reformation, statutes became far more closely worded and accurately drafted, but it is doubtful whether the scope for judicial interpretation was lessened. Justice Bromley, in Mary's reign, said of statutory interpretation, 'It is most reasonable to expound the words which seem contrary to reason according to good reason and equity', and later Sir Edward Coke was to make an even more outspoken claim for the superiority of natural law to statute. Sixteenth-century practice, therefore, seems some way from the modern doctrine of sovereignty as expounded by Blackstone that 'if the parliament will positively enact a thing to be done that is unreasonable, I know of no power on earth that can control it' (*Commentaries*, i, **91**).

It has often been suggested that during Henry's reign, Parliament was not so much sharing in law-making as being used as a useful instrument for adding weight to powers and decisions of the crown. An interesting example of this is the question of the succession. The king certainly made his own rules about the succession, but he always used statute to give his decisions respectability. The Succession Act of 1534 gave Parliament a new type of omnipotence in allowing it to name the exact order of succession to the throne. Following the precedent of Richard III, who in 1484 had declared Edward IV's marriage to Elizabeth Woodville invalid and their issue illegitimate, Mary would have been explicitly bastardised, but she was not, although she was barred from the succession. It was not until the Succession Act of 1536 ,which fixed the succession in Jane Seymour's children, that Mary and now also Elizabeth were declared illegitimate. This Act also extended Henry's power by allowing him to name his successor by will, should his legitimate issue fail. As matters turned out, Henry again used a Succession Act in 1544 to legitimate Mary and Elizabeth and gave them the succession after Edward and his heirs. This settlement was repeated in Henry's will, and if his children's lines all failed, the succession was to go to the heir of his younger sister, Mary (the Suffolk line) (**94**).

If the king really was only concerned with power, he could have depended on proclamation and ruled by edict. The Proclamations Act of 1539 has sometimes been interpreted as an attempt to establish an alternative to statute more directly under royal control, but this is a misrepresentation. There is nothing sinister in Henry's use of proclamations, which were a necessary method of making law for emergencies that occurred between parliaments [**doc. 15**]. They were accepted as having the same force as statute both before and after 1539. The object of the Act of 1539 was to dispel any doubts that proclamations were legal and to establish machinery for their enforcement (**80**). The way in which proclamations could be used in conjunction with statute has been shown in the pricing of meat. Throughout the 1530s the practice was that statute was used for major meat legislation and proclamations were used either by the authority of statute, or used simply to meet a particular emergency situation, where action could not be delayed. In 1536, when it was wished to suspend the policy of price-fixing for meat, it was done by statute, although order by proclamation was permitted under an act of 1534. The pattern of legislation in this case seems to demonstrate Thomas Cromwell's preference for statute where it was at all possible (**86**).

Statute was therefore the dominant law and king and Parliament participated in making it. There appears to be no good reason for doubting Henry's sincerity, when he talked of the union of king and Parliament in one body politic. He might have been the dominant partner, but he was in no doubt about the dignity of Parliament. Henry said to the judges and Commons in 1542, "Further, we be informed by our judges that we at no time stand so highly in our estate royal as in the time of Parliament, wherein, we as head and you as members are conjoined and knit together in one body politic" [**doc. 24**].

MANAGEMENT

Although there was considerable harmony between king and Parliament in Henry VIII's reign, there were matters which aroused great feeling. One of these was the question of money and the example of the 1523 Parliament showed the dissent that could arise if matters were not handled with tact and consideration. At this Parliament, Wolsey asked them for a subsidy amounting to one-fifth of their wealth and when asked to moderate his demand, Edward Hall reports him to have said that 'he would rather have his tongue plucked out of his head with a pair of pincers, than to move the king to take any less sum'. During the Reformation Parliament and in later parliaments there are indications that the king and the Council were making efforts to manage parliament, but there were very few examples of packing, dictation or coercion.

In the management of elections, there was one blatant example of dictation in the Canterbury election of 1536, when the Mayor, Sheriff and Commons of Canterbury were asked by Thomas Cromwell to cancel the first election 'forasmuch as the king's pleasure and commandment is that Robert Darknell and John Bryges should be elect and chosen citizens or burgesses for that city'. There is no other case like this and it is probable that there were some unusual factors involved about which no evidence remains. In normal circumstances, electoral management was very similar to what it became in the eighteenth century. When Thomas Cromwell sought election to the Commons in 1529, he and his friends had to make enquiries among those who had control over seats. Even in the borough seats, it seems that the best hope of success was to win the favour of the king or of an influential nobleman like the Duke of Norfolk. As the king's leading minister, Cromwell went to great trouble to scrutinise the by-elections to the Reformation

Parliament in 1534. In 1539 he promised the king that 'I and other your dedicate councillors be about to bring all things so to pass that your Majesty had never more tractable Parliament'. Their efforts amounted to no more than writing letters to shire magnates or owners of rotten boroughs like Gatton in Surrey, asking them to consider nominating court men.

It is not surprising, therefore, to read that the parliament was seen by some contemporaries as a council of king's men, though it is not necessary to go as far as Chapuys, who told Charles V of Catherine of Aragon's belief that Henry held the Commons in his hand, adding that they had been bribed and won over. Edward Hall, who was a member of the Reformation Parliament, said that the most part of the Commons were 'the kynges servaintes', while the rebels of the Pilgrimage of Grace, speaking at the meeting at Pontefract in 1536 said that 'if they should be truly named, they should be called councils of the king's appointment and not parliaments'. The councillors in the Commons, who chose to sit there and be active rather than sit as observers in the Lords, guided the House in debate and also helped to prepare parliamentary business. Cromwell, in particular, took on the task of drafting bills and lobbying opinion, but his were by no means the only corrections in parliamentary drafts.

The king had other means of influencing parliament. The Speaker, who took the chair in the House of Commons and was responsible for procedure and the order of debate, was always at this time a king's man. He was elected by the Commons at the opening of Parliament, but he was invariably someone who would meet with the king's favour. This meant that the king could always be sure of a hearing for his councillors in the House. The king was also in the habit of intervening on his own initiative. A letter written to the Mayor of Plymouth in 1536 told of the king delivering a bill to the House 'which he desired them to weigh in conscience and not to pass it because he gave it in'. This, if true, was a most uncharacteristic intervention. He used various forms of intimidation to force through a law on uses. In 1532 he threatened them that he would 'serche out the full extremitie of the law'. Meeting with no success on this occasion, he gained his way in 1536 by playing on the common lawyers' jealousy of the Court of Chancery, which was cornering all the litigation over uses. He also encountered opposition to the Bill of Annates in 1532, but he overcame it in the

Commons by ordering an open division, which frightened many of the opponents of Annates into joining the 'yeas' for fear of the king's indignation. His most usual tactic, however, was to call a deputation of the Commons into his presence as a propaganda exercise. It was at such a meeting that the king informed those present that the bishops were only half his subjects. This was part of the king's campaign of nerves to force the Submission of the Clergy (1532).

Opposition in the Commons was mainly confined to matters concerning money or land. Apart from the opposition to Wolsey's taxation in 1523, there was some criticism of the bill of repudiation in 1529, which cancelled the king's obligation to repay money which Wolsey had borrowed by forced loan. Hall says that the bill was 'sore argued' and he described the speech of John Petyt, a City member, who was not worried on his own behalf, but was concerned for the people who had borrowed to lend to the King. Opposition to the Bill of Uses was always vociferous. Hall, a keen supporter of the king, said of the opposition to such a bill in 1532, 'Lord, how ignorant persones were greved and howe shamefully they spake of the byll and of the Kinges learned council'. Yet on the whole, opposition was confined to occasional words and certain individuals. A good example of such an individual was Sir George Throckmorton, who opposed the conditional restraint of Annates, the Appeals Act and the king's marriage to Anne Boleyn. He was the leader of a small opposition group in Commons who used to meet at the Queen's Head Tavern. On Cromwell's advice he sometimes stayed away from parliaments in a mood of contrition, but was never quite silenced. After the Pilgrimage of Grace, he spent some time in the Tower. This kind of opposition was irritating rather than dangerous and the reprisals against them were never over-vindictive. Cromwell had shown that he was capable of opposition when he wrote a speech opposing the king's foreign policy in 1523, but he probably never delivered it [**doc. 7**]. This kind of individual opposition to matters of state was not considered dangerous unless it came from people high in public service, like More and Fisher, or if it coincided with a period of rebellion as in 1536.

PRIVILEGE

There are great contrasts in the descriptions of the freedom of debate during Henry's reign. Chapuys said that no man there dare open his mouth against the will of the King and Council, while Bishop Gardiner, speaking in 1547, but referring to a speech he made during Henry's reign, referred to 'the Parliament House, where was free speech without danger'. On the whole, it seems clear that there were enough common interests between king and parliament for the king to extend their traditional privileges considerably.

Members of medieval parliaments had been free from arrest at a private suit so that the king should not be deprived of their advice. The freedom of speech that medieval Speakers requested was for themselves only. They asked that Speakers should be granted free access to the king to convey the Commons' views, free speech in expressing them and pardon for any misrepresentation that might occur. A request for these privileges was made by the Speaker at the opening of parliament and graciously granted by the king.

Considerable extensions were made in the definition of free speech during Henry's reign starting with Strode's case in 1513. Richard Strode, a Devonshire burgess, had been fined and imprisoned by the Stannary Courts for promoting a bill hostile to the tin interests, but he was freed on the basis that the deliberations of the High Court of Parliament were privileged against action by inferior courts. A more substantial step forward was made by Sir Thomas More as Speaker in 1523. In his petition for free speech at the opening of Parliament, he requested freedom of speech on the floor of the House of Commons for the first time. It was suggested within a lengthy explanation that 'so many men boisterous and rude in language, see deep indeed, and give right substantial counsel', and he was really requesting a favourable interpretation of what was said. 'And whatsoever happen any man to say, that it may like your noble majesty of your inestimable goodness to take all in good part, interpreting every man's words, how uncomely soever they be couched, to proceed of good zeal toward the profit of your realm and honour of your royal person.' It was certainly not a request for licence for members to speak their minds. The 1523 Parliament turned out to be one of the more outspoken of the reign, but in general Henry respected the Commons' right to speak freely.

There was also an extension of Commons' control over the arrest of their members. Previously, it was the convention that the Speaker either started a bill for the member's release or requested the Court of Chancery to issue a writ of privilege to the jailer, which was in the nature of an order for the prisoner's release. In Ferrers's case, 1542, the Commons took matters into their own hands (**93**). They sent their own serjeant-at-law to demand Ferrers's release on the authority of his mace. When he was rebuffed, they gained the sympathy of the Lords and tried again. This time they were successful, but they took matters further into their own hands by imprisoning the offending city officials for two days. George Ferrers was burgess for Plymouth. He was arrested for a debt for which he was surety; he was also a page of the king's chamber. It is difficult to know whether it was sympathy for his servant or for his high court that moved Henry to allow these precedents. Both are mentioned in his speech to the judges and Commons. He confirmed the similar privilege for members' servants and interpreted the offence against Ferrers as one 'against our person and the Whole Court of Parliament' [**doc. 24**].

Commons also extended its control over its own members. An Act of 1515 gave the Speaker and Commons control over attendance. Any members wishing to go home before the end of the parliamentary session had to secure a licence from the Speaker and Commons. This meant that the House of Commons was exercising an independent executive function for the first time (**51**). They could now lay claim to being a court in their own right, capable of trying disputes which touched their own interests. By the middle of the sixteenth century, the Commons had established its claim to decide whether a person was qualified for membership of the House.

The whole growth of parliamentary privilege, which was to continue and increase up to the Civil War, was an indication of Commons' growing self-confidence. Precedents had been secured for the functioning of Commons as a court, for the enforcement of their own writs of privilege and for a much wider definition of free speech. If the king was making use of the partnership with parliament for the exercise of his own power, the House of Commons was also using it to establish their status as an independent court.

5 Theoretical Justification

The necessity of nullifying his marriage to Catherine of Aragon and his desire to marry Anne Boleyn led Henry to make greater and greater claims for his own authority against that of the Pope. As he was a firm Catholic and wanted his subsequent offspring to be accepted as rightful heirs to the throne, he was keen to have papal approval for his remarriage, but the more unlikely this became, the more he was forced to question the Pope's jurisdiction in England. Finally he repudiated papal authority altogether.

In the period between 1527 and 1532, Henry was first concerned with questioning the validity of Julius II's dispensation and then with the Pope's right to conduct the hearing of his case in Rome. Up to this point pressure had been brought on the Church in England, but no measures had been taken against the Pope. Direct pressure on Rome began with the Act in Conditional Restraint of Annates 1532, and it was accompanied by a propaganda campaign, which became more extreme, as pressure on the Papacy increased. Most of the books supporting Henry's case were published by the royal printer, Thomas Berthelet and therefore had some kind of official approval.

A considerable variety of books were published. Some were pamphlets aimed at a wide audience, like the anonymous *A Glasse of the Truth* (1532), others like Fox's *De Vera Differentia* (1534) and Gardiner's *De Vera Obedientia* (1535) were written in Latin for the educated public both at home and abroad. Attempts to find English medieval treatises defending royal supremacy were vain as the only examples were those of Wycliffe and the Lollards which were heretical, but the gap was filled by translations of the works of Marsiglio of Padua, a fourteenth-century Italian, with the adverse chapters omitted. St German published a series of works between 1530 and 1535 which would have mainly appealed to lawyers. In addition to these, there were court writers like Thomas Starkey and Richard Morison, both of whom had been members of Reginald Pole's humanist circle at Padua, and managed to avoid being associated with Pole's opposition to Henry's remarriage.

There was no great coherence in the ideas that these writers put forward. Their main concern was to justify royal authority against that of the Pope and to commend passive obedience. It is, therefore, not to be expected that their statements on royal sovereignty would be utterly consistent. They were not very concerned about sovereignty nor were they particularly concerned about the exact distribution of power within the partnership of king and parliament. These matters only became important when parliament and king were trying to defend their position against each other in the seventeenth century. During Henry's reign, they agreed that the power of Church and Pope should be curtailed, and this was reflected in the books that were published. After 1529 supervision of book publishing passed from the Church to the Privy Council and in 1536, 1538 and 1546 proclamations were issued strengthening royal control, especially over the importation of foreign books. In these circumstances, most works of opposition never passed the manuscript stage (**24**).

THE DIVORCE

The divorce needed justification, but it did not receive it in published form until *A Glasse of the Truth* was published in 1532. Previously Henry had been conducting a personal debate with the Pope in an attempt to persuade the Curia that Julius II had gone beyond his authority in issuing the original dispensation in 1505 [**doc. 2**]. One argument that Henry used was that the grounds given for the original dispensation were insufficient in that it was given only 'for preserving the peace between the crowns of England and Spain'. This argument was made untenable by the discovery of a second copy of the dispensation in Spain in 1528, which stated that it was for this 'and other reasons', and therefore this argument had lost all validity by 1532. The other main contention was that Henry's marriage to Catherine broke the divine law and that the Pope could not release anyone from this. This point of view was still strongly defended in 1532 and a long list of ancient authors was given to justify the claim. A scriptural text was quoted as further evidence. Jesus said to the Pharisees, "Why do you break or transgress the commandment of God for your own traditions" (Matthew

15:3). The scriptures were not a sure basis of support for the king, because the condemnation of his marriage in Leviticus (Leviticus 20:21) is contradicted by the order in Deuteronomy that a man should marry his brother's widow if she is childless (Deuteronomy 15:5). The pamphleteer of 1532 explains this away by declaring that Deuteronomy referred to the Jews only and 'should not be but in a mystical sense observed by us Christian men'.

The hollowness of the arguments in *A Glasse of the Truth* reveals the insuperable task that Henry had undertaken in questioning the authority of the Papacy to interpret the divine law. It was not only that to a papalist, a Pope could not be mistaken when he interpreted the canon law, but also that Julius II had many clear, recent precedents for issuing dispensations from the laws against marriages with kinsmen in the first degree collateral of affinity. There were also recent cases, where Popes had released Henry's relatives from marriages due to pre-contracts rather than to affinity, but the success of his sister Margaret in 1527 and his brother-in-law the Duke of Suffolk in 1528 in gaining release from their marriages, must have lulled Henry into thinking that it would not be difficult.

Had he taken sound legal advice in 1527, Henry would have seen that it was better to base his case on the insufficiency of Julius II's bull rather than on its illegality. Julius II's bull suggested that the marriage between Catherine and Arthur, which ended after five months with the death of Arthur from consumption, might have been consummated. The words *forsan consummatum* were used. This was important because a different kind of dispensation was needed for release from a mere contract without consummation than from a marriage that was both ratified and consummated. Only the latter created an impediment of affinity and it was from such an impediment that Henry VIII was released. If the impediment was of the former kind, which is called an impediment of public honesty, then a different dispensation from the one that Julius II had granted was needed. If he had argued, therefore, that the dispensation was valid but irrelevant to his particular case, there would have been no need to question papal authority. The Spanish copy of the dispensation would have helped him, as it stated categorically that the marriage was consummated. Catherine's insistence on her virginity at the time of her marriage to Henry would have been additional favourable evidence. Chapuys, reporting to Charles V on a conversation he had had with the king in

1533, said: "I urged that Henry had oftentimes confessed that the Queen was a virgin and he could not deny it, he admitted it, saying it was spoke in jest." Perhaps he could have been hiding the truth, as the evidence for Arthur's consummation of the marriage is far from substantial [**doc. 3**].

Wolsey seems to have seen the point, expecially when Catherine became 'stiff and obstinate'. The decision to base the case on Leviticus was taken by Henry himself and he thought that, if his case was to hold, he had to prove consummation. The English court had insisted on consummation at the time of the original dispensation, so this line also had the virtue of consistency. Wolsey accepted Henry's directives and sought to use Pope Clement VII's captivity in Rome after its sacking by imperial troops in May 1527, as a reason for summoning an independent council at Avignon under his own control as papal legate. This scheme failed, when only one Italian and three French cardinals attended, not at Avignon, but at Compiègne. The sack of Rome made Henry's task much more difficult, as the Pope was now the prisoner of Emperor Charles V, Catherine's nephew, who opposed the nullification of his aunt's marriage. Already, Henry was following his own plans by sending William Knight to Rome with documents that would enable him to marry Anne Boleyn. Marriage to Anne presented a problem of its own, as Anne's sister Mary Boleyn had previously been Henry's mistress and thus in canon law Anne was related in the first degree of illicit affinity to Henry and a papal dispensation was needed. Henry hoped that Knight would bring back a dispensation, which included a nullification of Henry's marriage to Catherine, but in fact, the dispensation that he secured allowed marriage to Anne, if the first marriage was unlawful.

The next eighteen months were spent trying to persuade the Pope to establish a court in England to hear the case. Clement was very courteous but rather evasive towards the new royal envoys, Stephen Gardiner and Edward Fox, who were trying to procure a decretal commission which would enable the case to be tried and decided in England, without the necessity of further papal intervention. The best chance of success lay between December 1527 and July 1528 when the Pope was free, yet an outcast, living in the decayed old palace of the bishops of Orvieto and the French army under Lautrec was dominant in Italy. It was at the end of this period that the careful Pope dispatched Campeggio with a full decretal commission to England, but that was the height of Henry's success. It was the collapse of French power in the Italian peninsular ending with their final ejection after the battle of Landriano (June 1529), that accounted for the gradual withdrawal of papal concessions. The appearance of the Spanish version of the dispensation also delayed the hearing of the case in England from October 1528, when Campeggio arrived, to May 1529, when the council met at Blackfriars. By that time, Campeggio had destroyed the decretal commission and was seeking all methods of delay. In June 1529 the Pope signed the Treaty of Barcelona with Charles V and vowed 'to become an imperialist and live and die as such'. On 31 July 1529 Campeggio, following the Roman calendar, adjourned the council for the summer and before it could meet again, Henry had been cited to Rome.

From this time on the debate with Rome over the nullification was sidetracked into an abortive quarrel over whether the case could be cited to Rome and whether Henry could be made to attend. The real struggle took the form of a campaign to persuade the Church Universal that canon law was on the king's side. English and foreign universities were consulted with the help of handsome bribes in 1530 and royal agents such as Stokesley, Croke and Casale hunted down rare books and manuscripts to help Henry's cause. Some universities did support Henry, but it was for political rather than legal reasons. It was openly said at Ferrara, that they who wrote for the king had but a few crown a-piece, while those who wrote on the other side had good benefices. In the circumstances, it was a good result that eight universities, including the university in the papal city of Bologna, judged in Henry's favour.

This does not detract from the fact that Henry's case was weak. Most canonists argued that the first degree collateral did indeed impede by divine and natural law, except for widows of brothers who died without offspring, exactly Henry's case. There were five theologians, living or dead who upheld Henry's argument. Henry took the line of one of these, a fourteenth-century Dominican named Peter Paludanus, that the marriage of widows as practised in the Old Testament was allowed only by special divine dispensation, which was in God's gift but not in the Pope's but Paludanus had reverted to the orthodox canon law attitude before his death. The Old and New Testament were against Henry's position, especially Jesus's acceptance of the fact that it was possible for seven brothers to have married the same wife, as the Sadducees suggested (**62**).

Henry's succession problems were to get worse rather than better. There was always the Duke of Richmond, his illegitimate son by his mistress Elizabeth Blount, as some kind of male heir, but Richmond died in 1536, the same year as the Boleyn marriage collapsed and Mary and Elizabeth were bastardised. By that time Henry had carried through a new policy which involved a complete schism with Rome, so that he alone became the final arbiter of canon law in England and dispensation became a matter for the Archbishop of Canterbury's court. The pamphlet *A Glasse of the Truth* was seeking to justify a case that was already lost. It was in 1532 that for the first time, Henry claimed that Julius II's dispensation was invalid as the first marriage of Catherine had never been consummated.

ROYAL SUPREMACY

In June 1530 the papal court to hear Henry's matrimonial case opened at Rome. Henry's attitude towards it was that it should have been held in England and that he could not be summoned to attend it. He therefore used every delaying tactic to make sure that it did not meet, because he did not want the court to declare the legality of his marriage to Catherine. This charade did not end until his agents Edward Carne and William Bennet were recalled in July 1533, after Clement had solemnly condemned Henry's marriage to Anne Boleyn and had ordered Henry to take Catherine back on pain of excommunication.

Meanwhile Henry was searching out evidence to prove that matrimonial cases should be heard in the province and not in Rome. He justified his claims from legal precedent and from history, so that by the end of 1530 he was in a position to claim national autonomy in all matters except heresy and to define his own supremacy over the Church. It is, therefore, difficult to understand why Henry delayed for three years before cutting off England's legal ties with Rome. One explanation is that it was Thomas Cromwell who showed Henry how statute could be used to effect a final breech with Rome and that the king had no coherent policy before he was shown the way. Certainly many of the claims that had been hinted at between 1530 and 1533, were brought together into a coherent justification for national autonomy in the preamble to the Act in Restraint of Appeals 1533, which owes much to Cromwell's drafting (**81**). Another factor is that it was not until December 1532 that Anne became pregnant and it then became vital to make the heir legitimate. There is also evidence of substantial opposition to the king's claims of legal autonomy, not only from the bishops, but also from nobles. Twice in 1530 a gathering of notables opposed Henry's suggestion that Rome should be disregarded and the divorce settled once and for all in England and again in 1532 a group of nobles gave a similar negative answer to Norfolk's proposition that matrimonial causes belonged to the temporal and not the spiritual jurisdiction.

Henry's first line of argument in 1530 was that there was a certain *Privilegium Angliae*, a national privilege, to enjoy legal autonomy. This claim was based partly on the Constitution of Clarendon and Northampton, which gave the king oversight of the church courts and control of appeals to Rome, and partly on the Council of Nicaea, which had decreed that all causes should be settled by the metropolitan (archbishop) of the province of their origin. It proved impossible, however, to substantiate this claim by more recent precedents, which were all in favour of papal jurisdiction, despite all the ferreting of Carne and Bennet in the Vatican Library.

Another line of argument was that Henry was an emperor and enjoyed imperial authority. This involved the kind of claim that Henry made to the Pope in September 1530, that he was 'not only prince and king, but set on such a pinnacle of dignity that we know no superior on earth'. At the time of the publication of the *Assertio Septem Sacramentorum*, Henry had told More that his crown imperial came from the Pope, but by 1530 very different origins were being suggested. King Arthur had a special significance to the early Tudors, through their reading of fanciful historians like Geoffrey of Monmouth [**doc. 12**]. The claim that Arthur was called *imperator*, because he had some vague kinship with Emperor Constantine's British mother could be ignored, were it not for the fact that the realm of England is proclaimed an empire in the preamble to the Act in Restraint of Appeals by the declaration of 'divers sundry old authentic histories and chronicles' (**81**) [**doc. 13**].

A further justification was provided by the anointment of Old Testament kings by God's will to rule over priests and people, and the supremacy over the church enjoyed by the early Christian

Roman Emperors from Constantine onwards. Constantine, for instance, had presided over the Council of Nicaea, and Justinian, as Gardiner says in *De Vera Obedientia*, 'made laws on the holy trinity, on the Catholic faith, on bishops, clerks, heretics and other such like'. Both Bishop Gardiner of Winchester and Edward Fox, later bishop of Hereford, supported the royal supremacy along these lines and it led them not only to argue caesaropapism, that is that the head of the realm is also head of the Church, but also the divine right of kings. In *De Vera Obedientia*, Gardiner could write, 'By me (sayeth God) Kings reign, in so much that, after Paul's saying, whosoever resisteth power resisteth the ordinance of God' [**doc. 17**]. William Tyndale, in his book *Obedience of a Christian Man*, of 1528, had made similar claims for the king, when he stated that 'the king is, in this world, without law; and may at his lust do right or wrong and shall give accounts but to God only'. These are not, however, true definitions of royal prerogative in sixteenth-century England; they are merely the logical conclusions of arguments that trace royal authority direct from God (**7**).

The declaration of the king's supremacy by statute in 1534 reflected these arguments, for care was taken to make sure that there was no suggestion that the royal supremacy was conferred by parliament. The Act of Supremacy merely corroborated and confirmed the fact that 'the King's Majesty justly and rightfully is and oweth to be the supreme head of the Church of England'. Yet once this fact is accepted, it is also clear that much of the exercise of the royal supremacy over the Church was governed by statute. Already by the end of 1534, parliament had transferred to the crown by statute the control of appeals from the church courts, the appointment of bishops, the grant of dispensations, the visitation of monasteries and the supervision of Church law. The Act of Supremacy added to these the power to reform errors and heresies committed by the spiritual authorities. In 1534 Henry only had a statutory right to amend heresies, but in the following years he began to declare doctrine with or without parliament's approval and to issue injunctions for the maintenance of order within the Church.

There was, therefore, enough evidence from the practical development of the supremacy for it to be seen either as a gift from the community to the king, or as a gift from God to the king. This ambiguity can be seen in the preamble to the Act in Restraint of

Appeals 1533, where the first few lines talk of a sovereign national state or 'empire', whose people owe allegiance first to God, then to the king. Authority in this part comes from below. In the next passage the king is furnished by God 'with plenary, whole, and entire power' and here power clearly comes from above. These different attitudes to the origin of power were prevalent through the Middle Ages; the first, tracing power from below, originates from Aristotle and was given new meaning by Marsiglio of Padua, the second descends from the Roman jurists. Both ideas of the origin of power were extant in the 1530s. Thomas Cromwell is associated with the publication of Marsiglio's 'Defensor Pacis' in 1535 and Stephen Gardiner, like Wolsey before him, was trained in the Civil or Roman Law; it is no coincidence that they emphasised opposing interpretations of the supremacy [**doc. 13**].

The writer who gave most support to the idea that the supremacy was a partnership was Christopher St German. His main aim was to attack the clergy and the church courts, but in the process, particularly in two works published in 1535, *Power of the Clergy* and *Answer to a Letter*, he argues for parliament's right to legislate for the Church. "Should not the parliament, which representeth the whole Catholic Church of England, expound scripture rather than the convocation which representeth only the state of the clergy?" he asked. Henry did not subscribe to this view, nor did his successors, but later parliaments had grounds on which to claim that they should be consulted on Church matters.

During Henry's reign the main aim of the writers on the supremacy was to inculcate a doctrine of absolute non-resistance to the king. At a time when there was always a chance of invasion from abroad to restore the Pope's jurisdiction and there was also widespread traditional support for the universal Catholic Church, the first need was for strong monarchy.

THE CHURCH OF ENGLAND

The independence of the clergy was threatened from two quarters at this time. There was first the prevailing anticlericalism, which demanded the curtailment of the powers of the clergy in the church courts and the removal of abuses. Parliament had shown itself to represent this kind of opinion in 1512 and 1515 and this anti-clericalism was called into existence again by Henry in 1529, when the Reformation Parliament was called [**doc. 8**]. The second threat came from the king's widening definition of his jurisdiction over the Church.

By 1532 the clergy, through their houses of Convocation, had succumbed, by giving the king his title of protector and supreme head of the Church with reservations, and had surrendered their right to independent legislation. The king had used the weapon of *praemunire* to charge the whole clergy with the recognition of Wolsey's legatine authority, which was papal in origin. He had fined the Southern Convocation £100,000 and later the Northern Convocation at York offered to pay a further £18,840. In addition, Convocation was asked to recognise not only his supreme headship of the Church, but also his right to cure of souls. Strong representations by Archbishop Warham and Cuthbert Tunstall of Durham against these claims persuaded Henry to reword the claims so that the bishops could still hold to their interpretation of Church independence. The supreme headship was to be 'as far as the law of God allows' and the cure of souls was 'a care for subjects whose souls were committed to their charge'. This was a minor victory for the clergy, but a further blow occurred in 1532, when Convocation felt forced to surrender its independent control of Church law by the Submission of the Clergy [**doc. 11**]. On this occasion, Bishop Gardiner of Winchester, later such a wholehearted apologist of royal supremacy, defended Convocation's right to make law for the maintenance of their faith, as one which was 'grounded upon Holy Scripture and the determination of Holy Church'. His argument was to no avail and only served to lose him royal favour (**50**).

What had happened by 1532 was that the king had eaten into the *plenitudo potestatis* of the Pope. The Pope's power had been of two kinds, *potestas jurisdictionis*, which was the right to control all the temporal aspects of church government and *potestas ordinis*, which was the power to administer sacraments and teach the faith. In reply to Tunstall's objection to his new title of supreme head in 1531, Henry defined his powers very carefully. His temporal powers were to incorporate all *potestas jurisdictionis*, but *potestas ordinis* was to be outside his power. Princes and emperors would be subject to the Church as far as preaching and the administration of the sacraments were concerned. From this time on, Henry did not try to claim the spiritual powers of a priest or a bishop.

The bishops and clergy in their House of Convocation had there-

fore been subjected to royal authority before the breach with Rome
was effected. The clergy are sometimes described as the Church of
England in the anti-papal legislation. In the preamble to the Act
in Restraint of Appeals 1533, they are the part of the 'body politic
called the spirituality, now being called the Church of England',
who were to be interpreters of the divine law. They were still
capable of being seen as a separate body in the realm, but on this
occasion it was only for royal convenience. In the Act, Convocation
was made the final court of appeal for church courts in matters
which touched the king, but this function was removed and given
to the Court of Chancery by the Act for the Submission of the
Clergy 1534. It seems that the only reason why Henry was willing
to retain the idea of an independent Church between 1533 and
1534 was that he needed the Church's approval of his marriage to
Anne and it was expedient that, should Catherine appeal, the case
should not be heard in a court directly under royal control.

The most characteristic idea of the Church of England among
the supporters of royal supremacy was that it was the Church
within the national frontiers. Gardiner said, "The Church of
England is nothing else but the congregation of men and women,
of the clergy and the laity, united in Christ's profession" (*De Vera
Obedientia*). St German's views were very similar in *The Answer* and
both he and Gardiner argued that as church and realm were the
same people, the head of the one should be the head of the other
(**50**).

There was still a clear idea of a Church Universal within which
the Pope would have no more power than any other bishop. The
Bishops' Book 1537, talks of the worldwide church as 'this holy
Church, the very Kingdom of Christ and the very temple of God'.
Gardiner in a pamphlet, *Si Sedes Illa*, written in 1535, asserted that
England and her sovereign wished 'to be fostered and fed and
contained in the universal church, outside the which there is no
remission of sins'. There was no intention, as far as Gardiner was
concerned, that there should be any change in doctrine or form of
worship, but he gives no idea of how the Catholic tradition was to
be maintained without the Pope. There was certainly no conception
of the Church of England as an independent shrine of divine law
in Henry's reign.

A General Council of the Church was considered as an alternative
to the Pope and during the first part of the Reformation Parliament,

pamphleteers stated without qualification that general councils were superior in purely spiritual matters to both king and Pope. When there was a distinct chance that Paul III would soon call a Council in 1536, reservations were expressed that the king could not submit to a council dominated by the Bishop of Rome. In his pamphlet, *Exhortation to Christian Unity*, written probably in 1536, Thomas Starkey put forward the idea that a council was 'a thing indifferent' and not stipulated by divine law. Their decisions were to have no authority among the people of any country 'till they be confirmed by princely power and common counsell' (**24**).

There was therefore faith in neither Pope nor in General Councils by 1536. The Church of England was an autonomous community ruled by the king, but the prevalent conception was to see it as the Church in England, still firmly part of the larger Church. All initiative lay with the king and within a few years he had exercised his power over the monasteries, over doctrine, over church discipline and over the Bible in such way that the Church of England was an unmistakable independent entity.

6 The Reformation

POLITICAL REFORMATION

The Reformation in England was in two parts. Henry VIII achieved a political revolution in the government of the Church by instituting an autonomous English Church with himself as supreme head between 1533 and 1534. The movement for religious reformation also made slight headway while he was alive, but it took root during his son's reign. Mary reversed both sides of the Reformation as far as she was able during her short reign, but the party of reform was so strong at Elizabeth's accession that Elizabeth found it difficult to deny the reformers any of their previous achievements. Elizabeth's Act of Supremacy 1559 was more or less a confirmation of Henry's, while her Act of Uniformity 1559 approximated to the wishes of the Frankfurt reformers, who represented a brand of religious thought that had barely expressed itself in England by Henry's death.

The political reformation was achieved by a series of Acts which bridged the nullification of Henry's marriage to Catherine of Aragon by Cranmer's court at Dunstable in May 1533. Preceding it was the Act in Restraint of Appeals 1533, which prohibited appeals in testamentary, matrimonial and tithe cases from the archbishop's court to Rome. The final court for ecclesiastical appeals was to be the archbishop's court, except in cases involving the king, which were to go on appeal straight to the Upper House of Convocation. In the first session of parliament held in 1534, the fifth of the Reformation Parliament, four important Acts were passed. The Act of Annates disallowed the payment of first fruits and tenths to Rome and laid down the full procedure for the election of bishops and abbots, which precluded the procurement of papal bulls for the consecration of bishops. The Dispensations Act abolished Peter's Pence and said that dispensations and licences should now be granted at Canterbury, not at Rome. The Act for the Submission of the Clergy took away Convocation's right to legislate without royal licence and submitted existing canons to the scrutiny of a commission. It also gave the right of appeal from the Archbishop's Court to the Court of Chancery. Lastly, the first Succession Act vested the succession in the heirs of Henry and Anne, making it treason to slander the marriage and enjoining an oath on every subject of full age.

These Acts had cut off all links with Rome, but during the second session of parliament in 1534 loose ends were tied up. The Act of Supremacy confirmed Henry's headship of the Church and gave the crown the power to conduct visitations of the clergy. The Act of First Fruits and Tenths annexed episcopal first fruits and tenths to the crown, but also extended this exaction to all parish clergy and other spiritual benefices. All these changes were defended by a new Treasons Act, which made it treasonable to desire, even in words, any physical harm to the king, queen or heir apparent.

These changes met with very little opposition. Sir Thomas More and Bishop Fisher of Rochester were arrested for not taking the succession oath, which they could not accept because it denied papal authority in the preamble. Yet they aroused little support for their concept of the universal Church by their stand and subsequent execution in 1535. There were some saintly opponents of the supremacy among the Franciscan Observants and the Carthusians, who were willing to suffer death, but altogether there were only about forty-five martyrs for the cause.

Loyalty to the Pope mainly involved the clergy and the ease with which the change was carried through is explained by their attitude. Bishops like Cuthbert Tunstall of Durham and Stephen Gardiner of Winchester, who had shown themselves very capable of opposing the king's measures, when they threatened the clergy's independence during the praemunire episode of 1531 and the Submission of the Clergy of 1532, made no objection to the king's supremacy in 1534. In fact, each in his own way justified the king's action, Gardiner in his *De Vera Obedientia* of 1535 and Tunstall in his sermon on Palm Sunday 1539. Tunstall's support was particularly important as he was one of the best scholars of his day. Erasmus ranked him with More, Linacre and Colet. By temperament he was peace-loving and somewhat timid, yet he rarely hesitated, at whatever risk to himself, to make known his real opinions and to oppose the adoptions of policies of which he disapproved. He was, however, 'the king's subject and vassal' and this political philosophy led him, till almost the last, to bow to the express commands of sovereigns (**50, 67**).

Most of the bishops were of similar outlook to Tunstall and Gardiner, especially towards the end of the reign, when most of the newly created bishops held conservative views. These bishops are called Henricians because they reflected the views of Henry himself. A Henrician can be defined as a bishop who was catholic, yet who supported the schismatic acts of Henry VIII. This influential section of the Church supported the political changes in the Church's status, but wanted there to be no change in doctrine or practice. They disliked the idea of translations of the Bible that had not been made by the bishops themselves. Tunstall as bishop of London went to great lengths to hound down copies of Tyndale's New Testament and in 1529 he commissioned an agent to purchase all the copies of the New Testament direct from Tyndale's workshop in Antwerp so that he could burn them. Gardiner's idea was that if a translation must be made, it should be so scattered through with Latin words that the people should not understand it much the better for its being in English. In doctrine they would allow no divergence from the orthodox teaching on the sacraments, the real presence and purgatory and looked upon the return to absolute orthodoxy in the passing of the Six Articles (1539) as a triumph for their point of view (**27**).

Their attitude is a reflection of their background. The road to preferment for a potential bishop was through the royal service. Both Gardiner and Tunstall had been ambassadors abroad before they became bishops and obedience to the king came easily to them. They continued to be used in the royal diplomatic and administrative services after they became bishops, Gardiner as ambassador to France 1535–38 and Tunstall as president of the Council of the North, but this mainly reflected the attempt by Cromwell to keep conservative leaders from the King's Council.

Cromwell, the vicar general, exceeded all the bishops in authority, as he wielded the king's supreme power over the Church (**92**). Although he was not outwardly religious, his political solutions to the religious problems presented by the monasteries, by the shrines and by the English Bible did link him with the party of change in religion. Cranmer, the Archbishop of Canterbury, was associated with these views. His approach to religious problems was far more pragmatic than that of most bishops. He was always prepared to study the opposing point of view and sometimes changed his mind in the process. Cranmer believed in the doctrine of the real presence until 1546, but on other peripheral matters of Catholic theology, like the celibacy of the clergy or communion in one kind only, he was prepared to make concessions. As far as loyalty to the king went, Cranmer was a Henrician in every sense, except that the conservative bishops did not count him among their numbers (**61**).

The passing of the Six Articles in 1539 and the fall of Cromwell in 1540 mark the temporary collapse of the party of change. Gardiner and his political equivalent, the Duke of Norfolk, had forced their way back into royal favour and entrenched themselves, by securing the resignation of the radical bishops, Nicholas Shaxton, bishop of Salisbury and Hugh Latimer, bishop of Worcester and their replacement by two conservative bishops in 1539. In the same year the notorious Edmund Bonner became bishop of London. The Henricians were therefore firmly in control for the last seven years of Henry's reign, but so much change had been achieved between 1536 and 1540 that a complete return to the *status quo ante* proved impossible [**doc. 20**].

THE DISSOLUTION OF THE MONASTERIES

It was possible for large parts of England not to have noticed the political Reformation, but few would have failed to be touched by some aspect of the dissolution of the monasteries. In 1530 there were 825 religious houses distributed over England (502 monasteries, 136 nunneries and 187 friaries) and even if the actual dissolution of all these houses passed unnoticed, the land distribution that followed must have affected almost every village in England and Wales. Simon Fish, in his scurrilous attack on the clergy, *A Supplication of the Beggars* (1529), assessed that the clergy 'have gotten into their hands the third part of the kingdom' and the *Valor Ecclesiasticus* (1535; see below) suggests that from a fifth to a quarter of the total landed wealth of the country was owned by the monks. As the total population of all religious houses was only 10,000, it is no wonder that their property was vulnerable at a time when they were openly criticised (**72**).

The main motive for the dissolution was financial. A memorandum of 1534 in the State Papers shows that the nationalisation of all church property was being considered as a way to provide for the defence of the realm and an army to fight the Geraldine rebellion in Ireland [**doc. 16**]. Dissolution of the smaller monastic houses was no new idea. Thomas Cromwell had already helped Cardinal Wolsey to dissolve twenty-nine selected monasteries between 1524 and 1528 and just before his fall Wolsey was granted a papal bull which permitted him to dissolve all houses with less than twelve monks or nuns. There was also the example of Sweden, where Gustavus Vasa secured the conversion of a substantial proportion of Swedish church property by the Vasteras Recess 1527.

The scheme to attack first fruits and tenths was implemented first. As a preliminary to the enforcement of the First Fruits and Tenths Act 1534, a commission was appointed to carry out a nation-wide survey of clerical income. The commissioners were chosen from among the local gentry and higher clergy and by the summer of 1535, they had provided a record of every ecclesiastical benefice and religious house and these were incorporated into the important inventory of church property called the *Valor Ecclesiasticus*. This was immediately followed by a visitation of the monasteries by Cromwell's own men. Their visitation reflected the confusion of ultimate intention which existed in the whole dissolution process. The injunctions which they delivered to each monastery enjoined on the monks a severity of observance which would have been impossible for them to fulfil, while the *Comperta* or report on the monastery seemed intent only on publicising scandal. It was the ammunition for subsequent dissolution that the commissioners ferreted out and the way in which they purveyed these stories to Cromwell in their letters, suggests that it was these that he most wanted to hear. The wish to reform is also implied in the Act dissolving the small monasteries, which gives the impression that only the smaller monasteries with less than twelve inhabitants were guilty of the abominations described, while the larger monasteries were 'great and honourable (**41**).

The first dissolution, dissolving houses valued at less than £200 a year, only accounted for 243 houses out of a total of 825 and did not include any friaries. So far the scheme was ostensibly only a reform of abuses, but by 1539, when the Act recognising the dissolution of the larger monasteries was passed, the whole monastic ideal was open to question. This would account for the dissolution of the friaries between 1538 and 1539; they owned no manors, rectories or granges and held no property of great worth. A number of larger monasteries were dissolved for their part in the Pilgrimage of Grace and thereafter they began to surrender of their own accord, probably greatly encouraged by Cromwell's agents. Between April 1537 when Furness Abbey surrendered and March 1540 when Waltham Abbey surrendered, all the remaining larger monasteries were dissolved of their own volition. A few abbots were executed for treason for denying the supremacy (Woburn and Lenton), for implication in the Pole conspiracy (Reading and Colchester), or for robbing his own abbey treasures (Glastonbury), but otherwise there was little resistance.

Cromwell probably hoped to use the monastic lands as an endowment off which the monarchy could feed forever. Chapuys reported in 1535 that he talked his way into the King's Council by promising that he would make the king 'the richest that there ever was in England'. The total net income of the monasteries according to the *Valor Ecclesiasticus* was £136,000, which was more than three times the income of all the crown estates in 1536, but out of this would have had to be paid the pensions and annuities to the dispossessed monks and nuns. There was, in fact, never any chance that it would be used as an endowment income. As early as December 1539, before the last monastery had been dissolved, it was decided to sell off lands to the clear yearly value of £6,000. The real spate of sales did not begin until 1543, when much land was sold to pay for the war against France. By 1547 something like two-thirds of all the monastic estates had been sold, but these still continued to yield reliefs, wardship and other feudal dues. There was a negligible benefit to society from these sales in the form of six new bishoprics and a number of professorial chairs at Oxford and Cambridge.

The sale of the monastic estates gave the purchasers a considerable vested interest in the Reformation and this was one aspect of religious change that even Mary Tudor dared not alter. At first the main interest was in acquiring leases. The farsighted benefited by leasing monastic lands at favourable rents, at a time when heads of religious houses were more interested in the short-term benefits of large entry fines, than in fixing higher rents for the future. There were also the leases of the lands which the monasteries had in hand at the time of dissolution available for lease between 1536 and 1539. These leases were at first taken by people like the bailiffs of the monastic estates, whose shrewd purchases laid the basis for many a prosperous yeoman farming dynasty, but after 1535 more and more of the leases were taken by knights and gentlemen (**68,** ch. 5).

When outright alienation of land began in 1539, the amount of revenue which the crown and later lay grantees could hope to enjoy was limited almost entirely to the regular current rents being paid in the 1530s. Some resorted to illegal methods to raise rents, but on the whole, Tudor landowners were more intent on consolidating their land and their reputation in the county than on immediate profit. Those that benefited most were those who purchased land, which they had previously leased.

The effect of the distribution of monastic land was to increase the size of landed estates already in existence. There is virtually no evidence for the creation of a new capitalist class of ex-merchants on the land. Often it was the great noblemen and courtiers who reaped the benefit, by purchase rather than by gift of the crown. In Hampshire 40 per cent of the monastic land in terms of manors had fallen to three people, the Earl of Southampton, Lord Sandys and Lord Paulet. In Devon, the Earl of Bedford made an equivalent gain, but here, as in Lincolnshire, most of the land was distributed among a host of men already well established in the county. Many of them had also acquired the right to collect tithes or to present priests to livings, so that not only land, but also clerical income and patronage changed hands. While the power of the king was extended over the national Church, the influence of the squire was extended over the parish church.

RESISTANCE

The Pilgrimage of Grace was directly connected with the reaction against the dissolution of the monasteries and it created the greatest crisis of Henry's reign. The king had no standing army and was completely dependent on the loyalty of the shire gentry if the shire levies were to be successfully raised. In Yorkshire, at least, enough gentlemen and nobility declared for the Pilgrims for them to attract the potential militia into their own ranks. Families did not remain united in their defection nor did Pilgrims attract more than a cross-section of the northern gentry, but it was enough to close the North to royal influence for four months. Henry Percy, the sixth Earl of Northumberland, had already subjected himself to the king before the rebellion started, making the king his sole heir and surrendering his lands to the king in return for an income of £1,000 a year. His brother, Sir Thomas Percy, who was unacceptable to the king as an heir to the Percy estates, joined the rebellion and a number of Percy tenants followed him. Lord Darcy and Sir Robert Constable were persuaded to join the rebels, but their sons remained faithful to the king. Lord Latimer and Sir Christopher Danby brought the knights and gentlemen from Richmond and the North Riding, and Lord Scrope brought them from Ripon and the dales to join the Pilgrims at York, but Henry Clifford, Earl of Cumberland and Edward Stanley, Earl of Derby, who were the greatest nobles west of the Pennines, remained loyal (**66**).

The original rebellion broke out at the beginning of October 1536, at Louth in Lincolnshire, but there it never had the support of the gentry. The Commons, under their popular leader Captain Cobbler, proved unable to sustain the campaign of terror by which monks and gentlemen were forced into their ranks and the rebels were persuaded to disperse after a fortnight, just as Yorkshire rose in revolt. The leader in Yorkshire was Robert Aske, an able London lawyer and county gentleman of eloquence and intelligence. Inspired by Lincolnshire's example, he raised the East Riding and was joined in a march on York by similar movements in the North Riding and Durham. There were also separate risings in Cumberland and Lancashire. Faced with an organised army of 30,000, the king was helpless. He soon had armies in the field under the Duke of Suffolk and the Earl of Shrewsbury, but such was the lack of equipment and spirit among the soldiers, that they were not in a position to face the rebels in open battle. The best that the Council hoped at this time was that they could hold the fords on the River Trent; both Shrewsbury and the Duke of Norfolk felt themselves hopelessly exposed when they advanced to the River Don. Norfolk's report from Doncaster on 29 October 1536 was that 'it was impossible for his army to give battle or retreat as he had no horse and they had the flower of the North'. Certainly the northern levies were much better trained for war due to their experience in fighting the Scots.

In the circumstances, it was fortunate for the king that the Pilgrims were filled with high principles and loyalty to the monarchy, and were unwilling to use violence except in the last resort. The one common motive among all the rebels was the conservative desire to reverse the recent changes in religion. Everywhere the religious motive was listed among the grievances, but in Yorkshire it seems to have been the predominant one. Their first and last insistence was that the dissolved monasteries should be restored and this was maintained without any great display of zeal for the Pilgrimage from the monks themselves. The considered list of articles drawn up at Pontefract in December also wanted the part of the supremacy touching the cure of souls restored to the Papacy. They also wanted first fruits and tenths abolished, Church 'liberties' restored, heretical works destroyed and heretical bishops burnt (**41**).

Another strong complaint was that the king was being advised by people of low birth and small reputation, like Lord Cromwell and Sir Richard Rich. Cromwell was hated for his prosecution of the Grand Jury of York before Star Chamber for acquitting an alleged murderer. In addition, there were social and legal grievances. The gentry were concerned about the Statute of Uses which restrained them 'in the declaration of their wills concerning their lands', but the Commons complained of the loss of pasture right by enclosure and of high entry fines, which were proving impossible burdens in the valleys of north-west Yorkshire, Cumberland and Westmorland, where population was growing. Poverty was certainly a reason for popular unrest in an area that Norfolk described as 'the most barren country of the realm'.

The multiplicity of the grievances and the difficulty of coordinating widespread revolt in a common rebellion were problems for the Pilgrims, but it was their limited objectives which accounted for their failure. Their aim was to make the king change his mind by a show of force and in this they succeeded, for at Doncaster in December 1536, Norfolk gave in to all their demands, a free pardon, a free parliament and the restoration of the dissolved monasteries. At no time did either Norfolk or Henry intend to fulfil their promises and it was naïve of Aske and Darcy to expect them to do so. The Pilgrims' trust can only be explained in terms of their loyalty. Despite his firm support for the Pilgrims, Darcy declared that 'it shall never be said that old Tom shall have one traitor's tooth in his head . . . for my part I have been and ever will be true both to King Henry VII and to the King our sovereign lord . . .' and Aske also professed his loyalty right up to his execution.

A further outbreak of rebellion in the East Riding of Yorkshire, led by Sir John Bigod and John Hallam, in January 1537, gave Henry an excuse to withdraw his concessions. Sir John Bigod was quite unlike the former rebels in that he was a Protestant and a critic of monasteries. His declared aim was to defend the North against the royal punishment that was being prepared. After the suppression of this and a further rising in Cumberland, Norfolk subjected the West March to summary punishment under martial law and then he tried rebel leaders in Durham and Yorkshire by normal indictment and trial by jury (**52**). A total of 216 executions are recorded; among the victims were two peers, Lord Darcy and Lord Hussey, and a number of knights, including Sir Thomas Percy, whose death brought to an end the Percy menace in the North. In 1537 the Council of the North was established and was served by many of the exonerated Pilgrim leaders. The basic loyalty of the bulk of his subjects coupled with the cooperation of the upper nobility accounts for the successful subjugation of the North (**31, 35**).

The potential threat presented by the rebellion is illustrated by the Pope's dispatch of Reginald Pole, now a cardinal and legate *a latere*, to help and encourage the Pilgrims. Pole was a leading Yorkist as grandson of Edward IV's brother, George, Duke of Clarence; he could have turned the rebellion into a dynastic war with religious overtones, like the later French Wars of Religion. Pole was sent too late to succeed, but Henry recognised the danger presented by the last descendants of the White Rose of York. In 1538 he arrested Cardinal Pole's youngest brother Geoffrey and forced him to give evidence against his family to save his own life. On this evidence, Lord Montague, the cardinal's other brother, and two of his kinsmen, the Marquess of Exeter and Sir Edward Neville were executed in 1538 and Pole's mother, the countess of Salisbury was also executed in 1541. The king's brutality in these cases is a reflection of his insecurity; at no time in his reign did he feel more beset by danger than in the years 1536 to 1539.

RELIGIOUS CHANGE

On doctrine there was very little deviation from Catholic orthodoxy during the reign. It has sometimes been said that the 10 Articles of 1536 made concessions to Lutherans, but if this is so, they were concessions of omission rather than of definition. There is a certain similarity between these articles and the Wittenburg Articles of Melancthon published in the same year, but only in areas on which there was no disagreement. The one great concession is the omission of four of the seven sacraments, but the three that remained were declared necessary to salvation and were defined in a strictly Catholic sense. The talks with the Lutherans of the Schmalkaldic League were continued in 1538, but the points of disagreement were not discussed. It seems that the king had no intention of making concessions. Already in 1537 the *Bishops' Book* had been prepared as an elaborate exposition of the Creed, the Seven Sacraments, the Ten Commandments, the Lord's Prayer and the Ave Maria, for circulation among the clergy. The four sacraments had been restored even though they were accorded a rather lower status than the other three. The talks with the Lutherans broke down on the question of communion in both kinds, private masses and ecclesiastical celibacy, and in 1539 these were incorporated into the Act of Six Articles presented to Parliament by the king's command. These articles were absolutely orthodox and enforceable by savage punishment [**doc. 19**].

There was never any doctrinal vacillation in Henry's mind. He was prepared to go a little way towards satisfying Lutheran susceptibilities, if it did not involve important articles of faith, for the political reason that it was conceivable that he might need their alliance to balance a possible Valois–Hapsburg rapprochement. The Protestant-inclined faction was most influential at court during this period, but they could boast no success in changing declared doctrine. The Act of Six Articles was a great blow to their hopes and a great encouragement to the orthodox faction led by Gardiner and Norfolk. The *King's Book*, 1543, which was a carefully revised edition of the *Bishops' Book*, was orthodox and sometimes even anti-Lutheran (**49**).

The main religious changes were the result of Cromwell's Injunctions of 1538 [**doc. 18**]. The first set of Injunctions passed in 1536 ordered the clergy to discourage the use of images, relics and shrines: the second in 1538 ordered their removal. This resulted in the desecration of shrines and sanctuaries all over the country. The reliquaries of famous saints were emptied of their relics and the great shrines like that of St Thomas à Becket at Canterbury were smashed and the gold and precious stones sent to the Treasury. In this way the practices of the Church breeding superstition were removed and objects of major scandal like the Rood of Boxley, with its figure of Christ operated by mechanical means, were displayed to public ridicule (**27**).

The other major command of 1538 was that a Bible in English

should be available in every church for people to read. As early as 1534, the Convocation of Canterbury had petitioned the king 'that the Holy Scripture should be translated into the vulgar tongue' and 'delivered to the people for their instruction'. Colporteurs had been distributing Tyndale's New Testament illegally since its publication in Germany in 1526. The Protestant interpretation of certain words and the addition of prefaces in the later editions of Tyndale's Bible made it quite unacceptable and an official version was obviously necessary. An episcopal committee first attempted the task, but Cromwell was attracted by Coverdale's Bible, published abroad in 1535 as the first complete edition in English. Its publication and distribution in England was permitted immediately, and if Cromwell had had his way its use in every church would have been ordered in the 1536 Injunctions. Another version of the Bible, the Matthew Bible, written by John Rogers under the pseudonym Thomas Matthew, was also permitted in 1537, but it was felt that an authoritative official version was needed. The work was entrusted to Miles Coverdale, who revised his previous translation while drawing on other translations, and produced the 'Great Bible' in 1539.

It proved impossible to make sure that Bible reading would not lead to 'any common disputation, argument or exposition of the mysteries there contained' [**doc. 21**]. Revision was considered by Convocation, but it was Parliament who tried to limit its subversive effects by an Act of 1543, which stated that only noblemen, gentlemen and merchants might read it. This attempt at control was entirely ineffective and in 1545 Henry more or less admitted this in his speech to Parliament [**doc. 26**]. The English Bible had made it possible for ordinary subjects to appeal to a new authority in the resolution of religious quarrels and the government did not dare to deprive influential people of it. Once God's word was readily available in the Bible, it proved impossible for the king's word on Church doctrine to carry the conviction of ultimate authority (**28**).

Uniformity was already an important consideration and a willingness to make concessions to tender consciences so that there could be 'a firm union of all the king's subjects' was already apparent before Henry's death. The justification for the religious compromise was made by Thomas Starkey in his pamphlet, *An Exhortation to Unity and Obedience* (1535), where he draws on Melancthon's ideas. Melancthon had distinguished between things that were necessary for salvation and 'things indifferent' or *adiaphora*, which were doctrines and practices retained purely as an embellishment to religion. The first could be equated with the divine law and the second with human law. Starkey looked on certain ceremonies and traditions 'as things convenient to maintain unity, whereas they repugn neither to God's word, nor to good civility'. Outward order was a matter of convenience, not of conscience and even in the ten Articles only three of the sacraments were judged necessary to salvation (**73**).

The English Bible and the quest for uniformity within a less than rigid mould already promised to give the Church of England a national character of its own, but it was the collapse of the Catholic party at court which made it certain that the ultimate settlement would be Protestant. Katherine Parr, Henry's last wife, encouraged Protestant opinions after her marriage in 1543, while the noblemen who were latterly in favour at court, the Earl of Hertford and Lord Lisle, also supported moderate reform. The young Prince Edward was taught by tutors who favoured the new ideas and was left with a Council of Regency that patently favoured reform. Gardiner's name was removed from the Council, Norfolk was in prison and his son, the Earl of Surrey, had been executed. The foundations of the religious Reformation had already been laid (**44**).

7 Foreign Policy

THE FOREIGN POLICY OF THE 'DIVORCE'

The characteristic aim of Tudor foreign policy was to adopt a position of neutrality in the endemic conflicts between the Hapsburg Empire and the Valois dynasty of France (**48**). England was not strong enough in terms of finance or of manpower to challenge the might of either of these Leviathans alone, but she could benefit from the desire of each to win her friendship. The period of the 'divorce', up to the death of Catherine of Aragon in 1536, took away this benefit, as it was quite impossible for Charles V to contemplate friendship while his aunt, Catherine of Aragon, was being deprived of all honour at court. From July 1531 onwards she was actually banished from the king's presence and was left languishing, often without the comfort of her daughter Mary, in various provincial country houses (**47**).

The danger of intervention by Charles V on behalf of his aunt was very small indeed. Between the siege of Vienna by the Turks in 1529 and his successful conquest of the Turkish base at Tunis in 1535, Charles V was obsessed by the threat of the Turks to Hungary and to his naval supremacy in the western Mediterranean. He had to shelve the German problem by conceding religious toleration to the German Protestant princes of the Schmalkaldic League at the Diet of Nuremburg in 1532. It was unlikely, therefore, that Henry's treatment of Catherine and the subsequent break with Rome would demand much of his attention. He could have taken economic measures, by placing an embargo on English trade with the Netherlands, but this was such an unpopular side effect of Anglo-Spanish war, on both sides of the Channel, that a truce was made with the Netherlands in June 1528 so that trade would not be disrupted (**70**). Thomas Kitson was able to send at least one shipment of cloth to the Netherlands in every year from 1512 to 1539 without exception (**59**).

Francis I was very eager to capitalise on Charles V's difficulties and this included building up the alliance with Henry. Francis bore the full burden of the campaign against Spain in Italy, on which the success of the 'divorce' depended, and in early 1528 there seemed a chance that the French might triumph. The French enjoyed naval supremacy with the help of Andrea Doria and the Genoan fleet, while Lautrec gained the military initiative, driving the imperialists from Rome and shutting them into Naples. By autumn, however, the position had been entirely reversed by a series of misfortunes. Andrea Doria changed sides, Lautrec died and the army around Naples was struck by the plague. Lautrec's army capitulated at Aversa in September 1528, and in June 1529 all French resistance in Italy ended after the battle of Landriano. Had it not been for Charles's other problems, the position in the summer of 1529 would have been very threatening to Henry, as not only did Charles and Francis make peace at Cambrai in August 1529, but Charles had also made peace with the Pope at Barcelona in July 1529.

The continuing attempts by Henry to make the Pope nullify his marriage to Catherine between 1530 and 1533 were both half-hearted and ineffectual, as has already been seen, but in these efforts he did receive the help of Francis, who often seems to have taken them more seriously than Henry himself. The reality of Anglo-French friendship was signalised by another magnificent meeting at Calais between the two kings in October 1532, when Anne Boleyn was received as if she were queen. Francis then prepared the ground for a treaty with the Pope, which was to be sealed by the marriage of the Duke of Orleans to Charles VII's cousin, Catherine de Medici. The crucial meeting with the Pope was held at Marseilles in October 1533, but by this time Henry had taken matters into his own hands to Francis's disappointment. Francis was interested in the prestige of a powerful anti-imperial alliance, which would include Henry and the Pope, while Henry was only interested in making sure that Francis would not come to terms with Charles.

Henry's policy in 1533 was that appeal should be made to a general council and this was made clear to the Pope and Francis at Marseilles. It was the German Lutheran princes who entertained the general council idea with most sympathy, but negotiations with them in 1533 and 1534 made little progress. John Frederick, Elector of Saxony, asserted that the Schmalkaldic League of Lutheran princes had purely religious aims and he was not interested in political agreement unless it would lead to a common doctrinal front at a subsequent general council. An uncharacteristic alliance was, however, made with the Hanseatic city of Lubeck, which sought Henry's aid in putting their candidate on the vacant throne of Denmark. It must have been the hope that he would be their candidate that led Henry to sign this treaty in May 1534, as it was unlikely to forward his policy of befriending Lutheran princes. The alliance with Lubeck was a distinct move against the Emperor, as Charles had his own candidate and Lubeck was a Lutheran city, but at this time the Lutheran princes were unwilling to jeopardise the hopes of a favourable religious settlement with the Emperor that had been promised at the Diet of Nuremburg. In addition, the throne of Denmark was won by the duke of Holstein, a good Lutheran prince, who defeated the Lubeckers in the process.

The death of Pope Clement VII in 1534 created a new situation as his successor Paul III was reputed to be friendly to France. Moreover, the new Pope was eager to call a general council. For a time, Francis harboured the idea of a coalition against Charles that would include England, the German princes and the Pope. Charles V was so worried by the possibility of such an alliance that he tried to come to terms with Francis, promising support for the marriage of Francis I's younger son, the Duke of Angoulême to Princess Mary of England, or alternatively he was willing to offer Francis Milan on the death of Francesco Sforza, if he would give up his alliance with England. Henry did not respond to Francis's offers of marriage either for Mary or Elizabeth in 1534 and 1535, as he wanted to avoid any possibility of close alliance with France leading to war with Charles, which was Francis's ultimate intention. French hopes of a grand anti-imperialist alliance were dispelled when the Pope conferred a cardinal's hat on Bishop Fisher in 1535 and Henry replied with the execution of both Fisher and the other champion of the universal Church, Thomas More.

By 1535 Henry was so worried that a general council would be called by the Pope, that he took steps to avoid the possibility of its meeting. Another delegation was sent to the Lutheran princes in 1535 to persuade them to unite with Henry in a refusal to recognise a general council called by the Pope. John Frederick of Saxony still made clear that a religious agreement must precede a political one, but proposals for Henry's approval were agreed on Christmas Eve 1535. These involved thirteen Articles of doctrine, acceptance of the Confession of Augsburg and the conferring of the title Defender and Protector of the League on Henry.

These proposals were greatly criticised by Bishop Gardiner and were shelved, when events turned in the king's favour in 1536. The announcement of the death of Catherine of Aragon was received with unrestrained joy at court. 'God be praised that we are free of all suspicion of war', said Henry. The death of Francesco Sforza, Duke of Milan, in 1535, also led to a dispute between Francis and Charles over the succession in Milan, which made it possible for Henry to revert to his policy of neutrality. When the news of Catherine's death was given in a letter from Cromwell to the king's ambassadors in France, Bishop Gardiner and John Wallop, they were told, "Ye therefore in your conferences and proceedings with the French King and his council shall . . . keep yourselves the more aloof and be the more froit and cold in relenting to any of their overtures or requests" (**2**).

SCOTLAND AND IRELAND

Scotland presented a great threat to Henry throughout his reign, especially when he was at war with France. When war broke out between England and France in 1512, James IV of Scotland felt much more loyalty to the Aulde Alliance than to the more recent marriage treaty with England, even though he was married to Henry's sister, Margaret. The result of James's intervention in this war was his defeat and death at Flodden in 1513.

At his accession, James V was only seventeen months old, so there were strong hopes in England that his mother Margaret would control the regency and keep the anglophile party in control. Margaret was far too capricious to fulfil Henry's desires, and by her marriage to Archibald Douglas, Earl of Angus, she aroused the jealousy of the leading Scottish nobles. On their insistence, she gave up the regency to the Duke of Albany, who was heir to the throne and cousin of the king. Albany was more French than Scottish in outlook and his governorship of Scotland from 1515 to 1524 was a time of worry for Henry. Cromwell, in a speech he prepared for the 1523 Parliament, saw Scotland as the first priority of English foreign policy. He wanted to see it subdued and then united to England [**doc. 7**]. Henry's policy remained more limited than this while James V was a minor. He offered Scotland a sixteen-year truce in 1523 and a marriage between James and Mary, if Albany was ejected. When this was refused, an army under the Earl of Surrey ravaged the border in 1523.

After his departure for France in 1524, Albany never returned and James encouraged by the anglophile party at court, was proclaimed *de facto* King of the Scots. The French defeat at Pavia in 1525 set the seal on the triumph of the groups friendly to England, and Scotland presented no further problems during the period of the 'divorce' while France and England were friendly. It was the marriage of James V, first in 1537 to Madeleine, daughter of Francis I, and on her death, to Mary of Guise in 1538, that reopened the Scottish problem. This renewed close alliance between Scotland and France presented Henry with his greatest problem in the last years of his reign (**32, 39**).

Ireland always remained a low priority among Henry's concerns. He never felt able to supply the 6,000 troops that the Earl of Surrey judged necessary for the conquest of Ireland. The king's influence was confined to the Pale and depended largely on the cooperation of the two Irish families which dominated the lands round the Pale, the Fitzgeralds, earls of Kildare, and the Butlers, earls of Ormonde. Life outside the Pale was barbarous and backward. The clans of Ireland proper only recognised royal authority when a royal army was in the vicinity; they were used to defending their own land rights and cattle against their neighbours in war. When earls of Kildare were entrusted with the office of Lord Deputy in Ireland, they tended to participate in clan warfare for their own family ends and were called to London to answer charges of unfairness brought against them. More often than not they were restored between 1485 and 1534 as they provided a cheap method of keeping order.

Henry VIII was very keen that Ireland should contribute towards royal income and this is one explanation of his increased vigour in Ireland after 1534. In 1536 he took over the land of all people who were not resident on their estates, with the argument that their absence put him to the expense of sending over an army to Ireland. In the same year the process of dissolving Irish monasteries began, and in 1537 Anthony St Leger was sent over as head of commission to increase revenue and to reduce expenditure. One of the economies was that the Lord Deputy's garrison army was to be reduced to 340 men.

One way of increasing regular income from Ireland was found by persuading Irish families to hold their land from the king by knight service for a rent. This enabled them to pass their land from father to son instead of holding it from the clan. Henry also continued the slow civilising process of calling the clan leaders to his presence to imbibe the gentle atmosphere of the court. In 1540, for example, the wild man Tirlogh O'Toole, who bivouacked with his clansmen on the Wicklow mountains and had to be given £20 by the Lord Deputy to make the journey, spent a month there and became a king's tenant by knight service. Most of the visitors were rather less primitive. Con Bacagh O'Neill was induced to go to court to receive the earldom of Tyrone in 1542 and Murrough O'Brien made a similar visit to become Earl of Thomond in 1543. It was the view of Anthony St Leger, Lord Deputy from 1540 to 1547, that 'titles and little acts of civility weigh more with these rude fellows than a show of force'.

The anarchy of Ireland made it a potential area of subversion for Henry's enemies. Rebellion was always dangerous, as there was a tendency for rebels to appeal for foreign help. Such a rebellion was that of Thomas Lord Offaly, 'silken' Thomas, whose retainers wore a silken fringe on their helmet. He was son of the ninth earl of Kildare and was appointed deputy of Ireland while his father was in England answering charges. Thomas refused to go to London himself, but instead threw off his allegiance in June 1534 after the premature announcement of his father's death in the Tower. The Archbishop of Dublin was cruelly murdered and Dublin was besieged. The rebellion was contained as the Butlers remained loyal and Dublin was never taken. In October 1534 Sir William Skeffington landed with fresh forces and the war was quickly carried into Kildare country with the successful siege of Maynooth Castle in early 1535. Lord Thomas surrendered and together with his five uncles was sent to London for execution by act of attainder in 1537.

The Reformation was successfully carried through in Ireland by Lord Leonard Grey, Lord Deputy from 1536 to 1540. The Irish parliament was subservient except for the opposition of the clerical proctors from each Irish diocese, and in 1536 and 1537 the whole essence of Henry's reformation was accepted, including the dissolution of the monasteries. By 1547 most of the leading bishops and clan leaders had sworn their acceptance of the royal supremacy, but there was no great desire for any outward religious change. Archbishop Browne of Dublin felt that he was acting alone in his attempts to dispel superstitious practices. In particular he resented the lack of support from Lord Grey, of whom he said, 'I think the simplest holy water clerk is better esteemed than I am'. Monasteries and friaries were dissolved only very slowly in the more remote parts of Ireland and the friars, joined in 1542 by the Jesuits, were able to preach pure Catholic doctrine to the people. The Reformation remained therefore, only a surface phenomenon. In England, Anglicanism was the outcome of national independence; in Ireland it was the badge of conquest (**23**).

Between 1538 and 1540 Lord Grey made vigorous efforts to force the chieftains of western Munster, Connaught and Ulster into submission, but this was interpreted as mere rashness. He made many enemies by his insensitive disregard of advice and was open to the charge of favouring the Fitzgeralds, as his sister had been married to the ninth earl of Kildare. The charge against Grey was that he 'cannot find in his heart to love or favour any man that is preferred, favoured, or put in trust by his Majesty within his land'. As evidence against him accumulated, he was executed in 1541.

The Lord Deputyship of Anthony St Leger was a period of reconciliation. Malcontents were placated with the offer of monasteries and peerages and they accepted the royal supremacy. In 1541 the Irish Parliament granted Henry the title of King of Ireland, as a visible proof to the Irish people that the Pope was no longer sovereign in Ireland. Although this suggested an extension of Henry's lordship over all Ireland, in fact royal influence remained relatively ineffective beyond the Pale (**23**).

THE CRISIS OF 1539

What Henry feared most was an alliance between Francis I and Charles V to carry out the deposition order that the Pope had ready for publication from 1535 onwards. He had nothing to fear while France and the Empire were at war over Milan, but by 1538 there were distinct signs of a reconciliation. In June 1538 the Pope mediated the Truce of Nice, without ever bringing the two sides together, but Charles and Francis did meet with a show of cordiality in the presence of the Pope at Aigues Mortes in July 1538.

This Hapsburg–Valois rapprochement seemed all the more dangerous, as there were other problems at home and abroad which seemed connected with a concentrated Catholic effort. The Exeter conspiracy was unearthed in 1538 and in the same year James V bound himself once again in marriage to a French princess. Efforts by Henry to break up the Hapsburg–Valois entente by offering himself in marriage to various French princesses, even to the extent of suggesting that a number of them should be brought to Calais for his inspection, proved abortive. He also considered marriage with Christina, Duchess of Milan, daughter of Christian II of Denmark and niece of Charles V, but these negotiations failed in November 1538. In December the papal order deposing Henry was actually published, Cardinal Pole was dispatched from Rome as legate to rally the Catholic powers against 'the most cruel and abominable tyrant', and David Beaton was made a cardinal and sent to Scotland (**62**).

Henry took the possibility of invasion very seriously indeed. Since 1492, when the duchy of Brittany was annexed by the French crown, the French controlled the whole length of coastline on the opposite side of the English Channel. The ports of Brest and Havre de Grace were developed into considerable dockyards, so that with the help of the prevailing south-westerly winds, the French fleet could invade the south coast with wind advantage. This particular threat was well understood by Henry and in the French wars he concentrated his naval activities against the port of Brest. Neither in 1512 nor in 1522 was much achieved, but this was mainly due to the shortcomings of naval gunnery and tactics.

Henry went to great lengths to develop his navy. He inherited seven ships from his father and by 1514 had added twenty-four more either by purchase or construction. In 1539, when the crisis was faced, Marillac, the new French ambassador, talked of 120 ships in the mouth of the Thames and thirty at Portsmouth. Some of these were the large carracks with heavy castellated superstructures at bow and stern, others were flush-deck galleasses, armed with heavy guns and oars, so that they could act as a travelling battery, without being grappled by the enemy. The width of the beam of the ships was increased so that they could carry the guns within the hull of the ships and fire through ports cut into the side (**46**).

On land, the coastal defences were frantically repaired and improved between 1538 and 1539, so that every estuary and exposed beach from the Thames to the Scilly Isles was adequately defended by blockhouses or elaborately designed castles. Many of them were built with materials taken from neighbouring monasteries. In March 1539 the levies of the southern and south-eastern shires were mustered and put under arms, ready to withstand an invasion at the moment that the beacons were lighted. The northern levies had also been mustered by the Duke of Norfolk to guard the Scottish frontier.

The reason for the mobilisation at this time was the fear created by rumours of armies and fleets preparing in continental ports. An imperial fleet did leave the Netherlands in April bound for the Mediterranean, which anchored off the Kentish coast for a time. The atmosphere of crisis was heightened by the recall of the French and Imperial ambassadors in ominous unison in February 1539. It was therefore a time of great relief at the English court when Marillac was sent to replace Castillon as French ambassador in March.

Diplomatic moves were made to improve England's strength on the continent. In January 1539 new talks were opened with the Schmalkaldic League and in April the first Lutheran delegation arrived in England led by Francis Burckhardt, vice-chancellor of Saxony. Henry also made approaches to the King of Denmark and the city of Wismar. The Lutheran talks in London were entirely theological and made no progress; they were brought to a summary conclusion in June when Parliament passed the Act of Six Articles, which contained doctrines that the Lutherans abhorred. Henry also allowed Cromwell to negotiate with the Duke of Cleves. This move was calculated to alarm Charles V, as the duchy held a very important strategic position astride the Rhine and William, Duke of Cleves, was in dispute with Charles over the ownership of Guelderland. John, Duke of Cleves, who died in 1539, was father-in-law to the Lutheran Duke of Saxony, but otherwise was a Catholic of the same complexion as Henry. His successor, William, felt greatly in need of an ally against the Emperor and therefore consented to the marriage of his sister Anne to Henry in July 1539. By this time the crisis atmosphere had passed and there was no longer any compelling need for Henry to become involved in continental politics (**2**).

Within the next six months Henry had become entirely bound to Cleves by his marriage to Anne at Greenwich on 6 January 1540. The determination of Thomas Cromwell to have the treaty sealed, and the glowing praise of Anne's beauty that was given by Henry's agents, seem only a partial explanation of Henry's haste. There was, it is true, no relaxation in the vetting of Anne's qualities from June 1539 onwards, but the willingness of Henry to continue with the marriage seems connected with the permission given by Francis I for Charles to pass with his retinue across France in December 1539 to put down the revolt in Ghent. Such collusion, at a time when an imperialist army was active in the Netherlands, recreated the atmosphere of crisis that existed earlier. In February 1540 the Ghent revolt was crushed and there was no further indication of Hapsburg–Valois cooperation. In these circumstances, his marriage was both a political and a matrimonial embarrassment, for the alliance which it symbolised had a distinct anti-imperialist flavour, with which Henry no longer wished to be associated. Anne was therefore decently put aside with a sufficient household and an income of £500 a year, while Cromwell was made the scapegoat for a diplomatic aberration which was connected with the crisis atmosphere of 1539 (**70**).

THE POLICY OF WAR

The last years of Henry VIII were spent in war on the scale that stretched the king's resources to the very limits. Foreign policy between 1538 and 1547 cost over £2 million to finance at a time when the king's annual income was little more than £150,000. This kind of money was only found by substantial parliamentary grants, the sale of two-thirds of the monastic lands and the debasement of the coinage. No subsequent monarch before the Civil War was capable of sustaining armies and navies of the size that Henry maintained during these years. It was a time when England could match the financial and military capability of either Spain or France, if only for a few years, and it was therefore England's unique opportunity in the century.

Henry's self-imposed task was to solve the Scottish problem. He wrote a long paper before becoming involved in the war in 1542 called 'A declaration of the cause of war with Scotland', in which he justified the war against his nephew as one which was necessary to bring Scotland into its rightful subjection to the English throne. 'The Kings of Scots have always acknowledged the Kings of England superior lords of the realm of Scotland and have done homage and fealty for the same.' Henry also pointed out that he had tried to show James V that the two countries had a community of interests by sending Ralph Sadler for talks in February 1540 and by travelling himself for a meeting at York in August 1541 to which James did not deign to come.

French influence was very strong in Scotland and it was Cardinal Beaton who represented their interest even better than James's wife, Mary of Guise. War had broken out once again between Francis I and Charles V over Milan in July 1541 and Henry felt that France's preoccupation in Italy would limit French ability to help Scotland. The northern levies were mobilised in the summer of 1542 and Henry demanded that James should come to either York or London to conclude a treaty of friendship. As the Scots made no concessions, border incidents escalated into open war in October 1542. Almost immediately Scotland suffered both military and political collapse, when her army broke up in panic in the face of a smaller English force at Solway Moss in November and James V died from natural causes in December, leaving his six-day-old daughter Mary as Queen of Scotland.

Scotland's weakness in late 1542 was Henry's opportunity to unite the British Isles. He had influential supporters, who could represent his interests in Scotland, in the Earl of Angus and his brother, George Douglas, who returned to Scotland in January 1543 and Henry also placed his trust in the released prisoners from the battle of Solway Moss. Unfortunately the policies which they were asked to publicise were too extreme for most Scots to accept. The eventual marriage of Queen Mary to Prince Edward was the project on which union was to be based, but unfortunately the talk of homage and fealty owed to the King of England seemed a direct threat to traditional Scottish liberties.

The strong 'French' party in Scotland was led by Cardinal Beaton and firmly supported by the Queen Mother, the Earl of Huntley (Gordon) and the Earl of Argyll (Campbell). The middle ground was held by the Earl of Arran (Hamilton), who was next in line to the Scottish throne and was made Regent in January 1543. When Arran arrested Beaton in January and the Scottish Parliament suggested religious reform in allowing the use of the vernacular Bible and also appointed commissioners to negotiate a treaty with England in March, Henry had cause for satisfaction, but thereafter matters deteriorated. A treaty was signed with

Scotland at Greenwich in July 1543, which arranged for the marriage of Edward and Mary, though Mary was to stay in Scotland until she was ten. Soon after, however, Sadler reported that the English hold on Scotland had almost gone, that civil war was inevitable and that Henry would have to use force. Many Scottish nobles had been affronted by the ease with which the Douglases gained access to the Council, and Arran was very prone to move with the tide of opinion. In April 1543 the Earl of Lennox arrived in Scotland from France with supplies and Arran felt unable to keep Beaton under arrest any longer. The treaty of Greenwich was immediately denounced by the 'French' party and Arran felt bound to give up his support for Henry. In December 1543 the Scottish parliament denounced the treaties with England and confirmed those with France.

Meanwhile Henry had strengthened his position by allying with Charles V in February 1543; both guaranteed the other against invasion and agreed to uphold ancient trade agreements. There was also to be a major invasion of France within two years. In this treaty Henry expressed a wish to acquire Boulogne and three neighbouring towns; this is consistent with an obsession with the Scottish problem, as Boulogne was the French port of embarkation for Scotland and the Straits of Dover was the essential French route. Henry confined his commitment on the continent to 5,000 troops in 1543, obviously hoping that he could solve the problem before the year was out.

As the Scottish problem could not be solved by peaceful means, Henry had to face the prospect of war on two fronts in 1544. His plan for the 1544 campaign was the fulfilment of a new agreement with the Emperor in December 1543, under which two armies of 40,000 were to converge on Paris. To guarantee the Scottish border he sent the Earl of Hertford on an amphibious expedition to burn towns and lay waste the countryside so that a French army could not be supported by the Scots during that season. Hertford's attack in May was well planned and fulfilled its objectives, except for the burning of St Andrews, but it did not help the king's cause. Lennox had already come over to the king so that he could oppose Arran's claim to the throne, while Angus had already subverted to the Queen Mother's party. For the rest, there were more who were infuriated by Henry's wanton destruction than were impressed by his show of power.

In France, Henry made no attempt to strike at Paris, arguing that he could not move until Boulogne had been captured. Boulogne surrendered on 14 September 1544, but four days later Charles deserted him by making peace with Francis at Crépi. Relations with Charles worsened during the winter due to the privateering activities of British merchants, not only against French and Scots ships, but also against any ship trading with France. A number of Spanish ships were seized in the process, including the Spanish treasure ship, the *San Sebastian*, which was captured by Robert Reneger as a prize in 1545. Charles retaliated by seizing all English ships and goods first in Antwerp and later in Spain.

The year 1545 was a year of crisis when the musters were once again called out in the south, two other armies defended Boulogne and the Scottish frontier, and a navy of 140 ships waited in the Channel. The French expedition did arrive in the Solent in July, but Portsmouth was adequately covered and the French only managed a short landing at Bembridge on the Isle of Wight. The fleet then moved off to make another landing at Seaford, before being forced back to France by the outbreak of disease [**doc. 27**]. By 1546 it was quite clear to Francis that he would not win back Boulogne, and he was willing to make peace. England was granted Boulogne for eight years and France was to pay England a perpetual pension of 50,000 crowns and a further 95,000 crowns a year during Henry's lifetime.

The war with Scotland was not ended as the Scots refused to accept the terms of the 1543 Treaty of Greenwich. Henry's relations with Scotland had been embittered by the devastation of 1544, which was repeated in September 1545 at a time when the harvest could be destroyed. Moreover, the French proved far more generous in their distribution of bribes than Henry himself and they even landed an army under Seigneur de Lorges in 1545. Henry's one success was the murder of Cardinal Beaton in 1546 and the capture of the castle of St Andrews by the murderers. The castle was held until after Henry's death, but the fact remains that Henry's aim of subduing Scotland had failed dismally. His Scottish policy had drawn him into a war with France, which could well have been avoided and which brought England very doubtful benefit at a huge price.

Part Three

ASSESSMENT

8 New Monarchy

At first sight, the accession of Henry VIII seems to enthrone the epitome of the Italian Renaissance. His father, Henry VII, was buried in a tomb designed by Torregiano, replete with pilasters, puttie and classical medallions, and he himself was credited with many of the attributes of *l'uomo universale* by a Venetian diplomat in 1515. 'He speaks French, English and Latin, and a little Italian, plays well on the lute and harpsichord, sings from the book at sight, draws the bow with greater strength than any man in England, and jousts marvellously.' To these attributes can be added his skills in theology and musical composition [**doc. 4**].

The impression, however, would be misleading. Henry was no great patron of humanism and was responsible for the death of the most esteemed humanist of the age when he ordered the execution of Sir Thomas More in 1535. Also he gave no great encouragement to the aristocratic court poets, who adapted the Italian sonnet and Petrarch's technique to the English language. Henry Howard, the youngest and most gifted poet of the reign was executed for reasons of state in 1547. There seemed truth in More's assessment of Henry's character, that 'if my head could win him a castle in France . . . it should not fail to go' (**26**).

Despite Henry's lack of scruple in ridding himself of some of the most creative minds of his reign, both the study of classical Greek and Latin and the popularity of learning did increase. Learning had long been seen as the sphere of clerics, but scholarship now came to be seen as a valuable qualification for any potential government servant. A number of new colleges at Oxford and Cambridge had been founded in Henry VII's reign, usually by bishops who understood the value of classical studies, and the tradition was continued by Wolsey and Henry. Wolsey not only founded Cardinal's College (later Christ Church), at Oxford, and brought into it scholars from Cambridge with distinctly heretical ideas, but also supported scholars in the household of his bastard Thomas Winter, while Henry supported Reginald Pole's household in Padua, which became a home for talented scholars. Cromwell employed some of these Paduan scholars as court propagandists and at the end of his reign, Henry founded five regius professorships at Oxford and Cambridge and in each university one of them was in Greek. Greek studies were by that time already famous at Cambridge due to the international reputation of John Cheke.

Although there was no halt in the development of humanist studies after More's death in 1535, as R. W. Chambers has suggested (**26**), it is true that the leading humanists were not such prominent public figures as they had been before 1535. The most important change in the last years of Henry VIII was the acceptance of bookish education as a necessary part of a gentleman's upbringing. Schools like St Paul's, founded by John Colet in 1509 and made famous for its classical languages by William Lily, were unusual, but language teaching at older foundations like Eton and Winchester improved. The lost educational facilities of the monasteries were partially replaced by king's schools attached to cathedrals and increasingly they were asked to accept the sons of gentlemen (**64**). Whereas education in the fifteenth century was still predominantly a preparation of the sons of the poor for the Church, by Henry's reign it was becoming valued as a potential gentleman's preparation for life. As late as 1516, Richard Pace, a leading humanist, was told that 'all learned men are paupers. . . . Gentlemen's sons should be able to sound the hunting horn, hunt cunningly, neatly train and use their hawk' (**85**).

During Henry's reign, it became accepted that the only suitable preparation for court service was through a school and university education. Thomas Elyot, who described the ideal education for a potential ruler in *The Governor*, a book published in 1531, would not have approved of their motives. He recommended an education of the whole man, who, in the Italian ideal, would develop a rounded personality and a complete individuality, while what most gentlemen wanted for their sons, for purely practical reasons, was a knowledge of the law, gained perhaps at university or perhaps at the Inns of Court. Education was often described as a preparation for public service, and there was an admission that the claim of nobles to serve the public was not automatic and absolute. The main criterion for service was now seen as education and ability (**25**). Sons of gentlemen began to figure prominently not only in the entries to Eton and Winchester, but also to Oxford and Cambridge. Hugh

Latimer had spotted the trend when he said in 1550, 'There be none now but great men's sons in the colleges and their fathers look not to have them preachers' (**36**). The development was full of significance for the future, for it meant that the gentle class, which had already been given increasing responsibility in Parliament and local government, was developing an informed expertise.

In all western European countries in the late fifteenth and early sixteenth centuries, there was a new spirit in government which is given the name 'New Monarchy'. In fact, it was not new in any real sense, as it did not involve any new institutions; it merely involved the more systematic use of those already in existence. One characteristic of the new monarchies was their tendency to work through a small council of hard-working officials. From the administrative point of view, there was a retreat into the king's household, because the departments of state outside the household had been dominated by baronial influence. It involved a more vigorous exploitation of royal resources so that dependence on popular institutions like Parliament or the Estates General could be avoided. This kind of development occurred in the France of Louis XI, the Spain of Ferdinand and Isabella and the England of the Yorkists and Henry VII (**45**).

There were many practical reasons why kings needed to bring their peers into subordination for the sake of order, but in explaining the growth of royal power it is also usual to emphasise the theoretical justification for absolutism offered by the Roman Law, which laid emphasis on the sovereignty of the law-giver to the detriment of the customs of the people. Roman Law was perfectly familiar with customary law, but Emperor Constantine had denied customary law the power of detracting from the written law of the sovereign; it only had validity because the prince had not objected to it.

Though there was a reception of Roman Law in all principal European countries from the twelfth century onwards, England ceased to be influenced by it after about 1300. The common law in England displayed the same weaknesses of rigidity and slowness that were solved by the introduction of Roman Law principles on the continent, but in England the solution was found in an appeal to the king as the source of justice, which was his personal responsibility, and resulted in the emergence of new courts during the fifteenth and early sixteenth centuries, such as the Courts of Chancery, Star Chamber and Requests. Although these courts necessarily developed new procedures and borrowed Roman Law concepts, there was no danger that the common law would be superseded by the Roman Law, but there was a possibility that the common law courts might lose business to the king's prerogative courts (**37**).

The counting of docket rolls in King's Bench shows a considerable decline in business between 1522 and 1550, with a recovery thereafter. The reason for this was that the common law courts had lost control of litigation over land. The vast majority of cases in the Court of Common Pleas concerned debt, which was far less lucrative business. The popularity of the use as a means of avoiding feudal wardship on the inheritance of land meant that the litigation over real property was taken to the Court of Chancery, as the common law did not recognise the use. The loss of business was rectified by the Statute of Uses (1536) and the Statute of Wills (1540), which restored the law of inheritance to the common law courts. Even the loss of business to the common lawyers can be exaggerated as they began to infiltrate the new courts. There was never any distinction between 'a prerogative court bar' and 'a common law bar', so that lawyers could make their living in either type of court (**89**). In fact, a proclamation of 1546 ordered that 'no person who had not read in the Inns of Court was to be a pleader in the Chancery, the Common Law Courts, the Star Chamber or the Courts of Duchy Chamber, Augmentations, Surveyors, Tenths and First Fruits, Wards or Liveries, unless appointed thereto by the Chancellor or the two Chief Justices with the advice of the Benchers of the Inns of Court'.

Some, like Thomas Starkey, who had studied civil law, thought that the best solution was 'to receive the civil law of the Romans, which is now the common law of all Christian nations', but he suggested it for its legal content, not for its doctrine of sovereignty (**73**). There is a hint that Cromwell understood the Roman Law view of sovereignty. Gardiner, in a conversation with Protector Somerset after Henry's death, told how he was pressed to give a Roman Law definition to royal absolutism by Cromwell [**doc. 25**]. Cromwell was also accused of being a Machiavellian by Reginald Pole, another of his enemies. Pole made his case in a letter to Charles V written about 1539, when he reported a conversation that had taken place ten years previously, in which Cromwell had declared that Plato's idealism in politics, was outmoded and that he could recommend a book of practical politics, which Pole sub-sequently discovered to be Machiavelli's *The Prince*.

Machiavelli discounted all the limits of law and religion to a king's power and argued that whatever was necessary for the maintenance and development of royal power was permissible. It was a recom-mendation to a branch of sovereignty more awesome than that of the Roman lawyers in that it was aggressively amoral. Machiavelli, however, gained very little attention in Henry's reign. Richard Morison, the Tudor propagandist, remarked on this wisdom, but in his works the authority he used to justify his arguments was the usual one for the times, the Bible. The book which Cromwell recommended to Pole could have been *The Prince*, which was circulating in manuscript from 1513 onwards, though it was not published in England until 1532. In the absence of any statement on political theory or theology from Cromwell, it is permissible to see his life's work as the institution of a thoroughly sovereign monarchy, but it is difficult to reconcile this with his regular use of Parliament (**58, 82, 97**).

A. F. Pollard went too far when he praised Henry VIII as the architect of all the changes that occurred in his reign (**54**). It is doubtful whether Henry really understood the logical conclusion of his claim in 1515 that 'kings of England never have had any superior but God alone'. Certainly he did not intend to be the founder of Protestantism, nor is there any evidence that he pre-planned the breach with Rome. If he was driven to these extremes it was by necessity rather than by intention, and the planning was done by Cromwell, who in a very real way showed the way towards both the political and the religious Reformation. Whenever manage-ment of policy can be ascribed to Henry matters seem to go wrong. This is true of the divorce proceedings from 1527 to 1532 and of his management of foreign policy after 1541. Administrative reform, the shiring of Wales, the use of parliamentary statute and the dis-solution of the monasteries were all positive changes with a specific political purpose, and all of them can be credited to Cromwell.

In these circumstances, on what was Henry's contemporary reputation based? His chief ministers were always first and foremost his servants and he was rightly feared. He looked every inch a king, and it is the king moving within the pageant of the court which attracted the attention of the chronicler, Edward Hall. Cromwell himself described the king's majesty when he presided in the case of John Lambert, the heretic, in 1538. It was unusual for him to indulge in such eulogy in his letters, but this is what he wrote to Sir Thomas Wyatt in Paris.

> I wished the princes and potentates of Christendom to have had a meet place for them there to have seen it. Undoubtedly they should have much marvelled at his Majesty's most high wisdom and judgement and reputed him none otherwise than in manner the Mirror and Light of all other Kings and princes in Christendom (2).

Dressed in white from head to toe, symbolising an awful doctrinal purity, the king knew how to act his part (28). Henry was feared, not least for his vindictive and cruel treatment of any of his nobles or servants who were the least dangerous, yet he was capable of expressing a bond of affection with his people [doc. 26].

There were three political developments in Henry's reign which can be isolated; the sovereignty of king in parliament, the introduction of the modern bureaucratic state, and the extension of national sovereignty to every part of the kingdom. Each needs to be qualified and explained in the light of what has been written in this book. If there was a hint that Wolsey would have preferred to rule without Parliament, Cromwell welcomed its existence and widened its function. This was no doubt due to the common desire of Court and Commons to limit the power of the Church, but the sharing of sovereignty with Parliament in this legislation provided the precedent for Parliament's later claim to share in making all ecclesiastical legislation. Arguments for an intended despotism based on the Proclamations Act of 1539 are unacceptable, especially as Parliament proved so relatively pliable during the reign (87).

The barriers to despotism were insuperable in Henry's reign. It was not so much that the validity of statute was limited, in theory at least, by the need for it to conform to the natural law. The main limitation to despotism was the lack of a standing army and paid local officials. Without these, it was impossible to enforce legislation that met with the disapproval of the influential classes. The Pilgrimage of Grace revealed the limitations of royal power when it had to temporise in the face of an opposition supported by the local gentry. Laws, such as enclosure laws, which directly affected the interests of the country gentlemen were just not enforced.

For this reason it is difficult to see the validity of the concept of an emerging modern bureacratic state in the sixteenth century. Bureaucratic government needs more than just a clerk, a minute book and a court with a formal membership; it needs local agencies that can administer government decisions. The financial courts that developed between 1536 and 1542 would have had local officials to collect revenue, but no more so than the earlier household departments which they replaced. There was also a growing tendency for the Exchequer to farm out the collection of customs to private enterprise. If to this objection is added the ephemeral nature of the new financial departments developed under Cromwell's inspiration, the lack of cohesion in the formal Privy Council after Henry's death and the highly personal way in which Cromwell used his own institutions, the idea of an administrative revolution seems unacceptable. Household government was modified and lost its former flexibility, the office of secretary increased greatly in importance and the Privy Council became a formal recognisable institution capable of dominating and directing all the rest; all this added much to Tudor government, but it does not constitute a break with the past.

In the extension of national sovereignty over the whole realm much progress was made in Henry's reign. The concept of 'Empire' used in the Act in Restraint of Appeals had a distinctly Marsilian flavour and seems to claim the existence of a fully sovereign state in England, free from the jurisdiction of any foreign power. The idea of a nation state prevalent at the time was a legal abstraction rather than a living reality. The sense of community had probably developed no further than the legal concept of the community of the realm of Edward I's reign, when people accepted that they were bound together in obedience to the same law (**71**). The favourite simile of the theorists was to liken the state to a body, in which the government and the law was the soul. Rebellion was like a disease cankering the body [**doc. 22**]. So far as loyalties went, provincial feeling was still stronger than national feeling in the parts furthest from London. The Pilgrimage of Grace of 1536 and the Western Rebellion of 1549 can both be interpreted in terms of local loyalties and alienation from the central government.

The extension of royal control over the Church and the monasteries was a positive extension of royal power, as was the abolition of private franchises and sanctuary. Wales was brought under a similar system of local government and justice to the rest of the country and both Wales and the North were given councils, which provided the areas with readier access to royal justice. The efficiency of the Councils of the North and Wales were subject to the same limitations as other forms of local government in that they would only enforce those things that were not against their interests. The Council of the North, in fact, was particularly efficient during its first few years, keeping the peace, enforcing Henry's religious settlement and tackling the social problems of enclosure and excessive entry fines. Henry felt able to visit the North in 1541 and the rebellions of 1549 found no echo in the northern parts (**75**).

On the reverse side was the failure of Henry to extend his influence greatly in Ireland and his complete destruction of any community of interests with Scotland. In Ireland Henry achieved the outward marks of success by his enforcement of the Reformation statutes and the extension of sovereignty implied in the title of King of Ireland, but the Irish clansmen remained as much outside royal control as they had been before, despite the elevation of some of them to the ranks of the nobility. In Scotland the 'rough wooing' of the Lowlands had driven all Scotland into the hands of the French, except for those who had something specific to gain by supporting England. The clumsiness of Henry's handling of this problem left such ill-feeling among his opponents, that no peace treaty could be reached in 1546. Protector Somerset continued Henry's policy of bludgeoning the Scots into accepting a marriage between Edward VI and Mary, but even though he won the battle of Pinkie in 1547, Scottish recalcitrance was not to be overcome by defeat. No solution to the Scottish problem was found until the Treaty of Edinburgh 1560.

Much political and social change occurred in Henry's reign. The change was far more fundamental than anything that occurred under the Yorkists and Henry VII, so if the New Monarchy began with the Yorkists, it was completed during the reign of Henry VIII. What was really developed was the Tudor state based on conciliar government, which remained the government of England until 1641. Few of the tensions that were to develop in the system were manifested outwardly during Henry's reign, but all were there in embryo; the clash between the common law and the prerogative courts, the distribution of sovereignty between parliament and king, the divine or human origin of royal power, whether parliamentary privilege was enjoyed by royal grace or by right, and the clash between Puritans and Church. The real ingredient which was to promote disagreement was the existence of a new class of country gentlemen, experienced in local government, keen to be returned to Parliament and educated both in the new learning and the common law. It was they who could question the royal definition of power in the Parliament.

Part Four

DOCUMENTS

Documents

The extracts have been chosen to give a taste of the main primary sources for the reign of Henry VIII, with particular emphasis on the development of political ideas. Substantial extracts from political philosophers on the social theory side can be found in *English Historical Documents*, vol. v, *1485–1558*, ed. C. H. Williams (**5**) and in *A History of Political Thought in the Sixteenth Century* by J. W. Allen (**22**); on the political theory side extracts can be found in *The Early Tudor Theory of Kingship* by F. le van Baumer (**24**) and *The Foundations of Tudor Policy* by W. G. Zeeveld (**73**). *Utopia* by Thomas More is the best known and most readily available example of a work of this kind. Thomas Starkey's best known work *Dialogue between Pole and Lupset* can be found in the Early English Text Society Extra series no. 12, 1871, and Starkey's *Life and Letters* in the same Extra series no. 32, 1878. Henry Brinkelowe's Complaint of Roderyck Moss can be found in Early English Text Society Extra series no. 22, 1874.

Chronicles become a far more useful historical source at the beginning of the sixteenth century, as the chroniclers begin to record more than just lists of office holders. Polydore Vergil (1470–1555) in the *Anglica Historia* (**20**) began to apply the Renaissance techniques of textual criticism to his sources and produced a lively account of contemporary events. He expressed great animosity against Wolsey and although his account goes up to 1537 he is less valuable on the reign of Henry VIII than on the reign of Henry VII. Edward Hall (died 1547), who, unlike Vergil, wrote in English instead of Latin, is a better source for Henry VIII's reign, even though he often borrows from Vergil. He was a serjeant-at-law and a member of the Reformation Parliament, for the first four years of which he is an important source. Hall did not continue his history (**9**) after 1533, but left the pamphlets and papers from which a later editor could continue it up to the death of Henry VIII. Charles Wriothesley

(1508–62), was Windsor Herald from 1534 until his death. His *Chronicle* (**21**) begins in 1485; up to 1518 it is virtually a copy of another chronicle, but when he described events that he had heard about or witnessed in the City, he is a valuable source on public affairs. Raphael Holinshed (**13**) lived in Elizabeth's reign and tended to borrow from Edward Hall for his information on Henry VIII's reign.

The main source for government and state matters is the massive collection of *Letters and Papers, Foreign and Domestic of the Reign of Henry VIII* (**14**). This collection contains summaries of the state papers in the Record Office and much other material as well. It is possible to follow the whole history of the reign through this source. The more personal letters of Henry VIII, including his intimate correspondence with Anne Boleyn, can be found in *Letters of Henry VIII* (**15**). Much important material is also to be found in the *Life and Letters of Thomas Cromwell* (**2**) and the *Letters of Stephen Gardiner* (**8**).

Much of the contemporary material on Wolsey is hostile. This would include Polydore Vergil (**20**) and the political poems of John Skelton (**17**). *The Life and Death of Cardinal Wolsey* (**1**) written by his gentleman usher, George Cavendish, is a favourable account of his life with a very detailed description of his fall. The best recent account of *Thomas Cromwell* is by A. G. Dickens (**29**).

John Foxe (1516–87) has a unique position in the historical literature of the sixteenth century with his *Acts and Memorials*. It was published in 1563 as an uncompromisingly Protestant account of the events of the Reformation period, including the earlier history of the Lollards and soon became known as the *Book of Martyrs*. It can be accepted as partly reflecting Foxe's personal experience as he was a university student in the 1530s. John Strype, a historian writing at the beginning of the eighteenth century, printed some of Foxe's papers in his *Ecclesiastical Memorials* (**14**).

Substantial collections of documents on the divorce, many of them in Latin, can be found in *Records of the Reformation* (**16**) by Nicholas Pocock, and on the religious changes in Henry's reign in Burnet's *History of the Reformation of the Church of England* (**12**) edited by Pocock.

There are very few documents on administration in this particular set of documents, as these are more than adequately represented by G. R. Elton in *The Tudor Constitution* (**18**), which has a very useful introduction to each aspect of administration as well. There are many extracts on administrative subjects to be found in *The Tudor Revolution in Government*, by G. R. Elton (**34**) and *Tudor Chamber Administration*, by W. C. Richardson (**60**).

On the subject of Parliament the complete legislation of the reign can be found in the *Statutes of the Realm* (London 1816). The *Journals of the House of Commons* do not begin until 1547 and the *Journals of the House of Lords* are inadequate. The *Lords' Journals* for the Parliaments of 1512, 1514 and 1523 are missing and no journal for six out of the seven sessions of the Reformation Parliament exists.This dearth of material on the parliaments of Henry VIII makes Edward Hall's account all the more important. A collection of *Tudor Royal Proclamations* (**19**) has been published recently, much fuller in scope than anything printed previously.

The Union of the Two Noble and Illustrious Houses of Lancaster and York

Edward Hall, the author of a history with this name, is now accepted as an important eye-witness of Henry's reign. Hall's deliberate intention was to praise the Tudor dynasty.

For what noble man liveth at this day, or what gentleman of any ancient stock or progeny is clear, whose lineage hath not been infested and plagued with this unnatural division. All the other discords, sects, and factions almost lively flourish and continue at this present time, to the great displeasure and prejudice of all the christian public wealth. But the old divided controversy between the forenamed families of Lancaster and York, by the union of matrimony celebrate and consummate between the high and mighty prince king Henry the seventh and the lady Elizabeth his most worthy queen, the one being indubitate heir of the house of Lancaster, and the other of York was suspended and appalled in the person of their most noble, puissant and mighty heir king Henry the eight, and by him clearly buried and perpetually extinct. So that all men (more clearer than the sun) may apparently perceive, that as by discord great things decay and fall to ruin, so the same by concord be revived and erected. In likewise also all regions which by division and dissension be vexed, molested and troubled, be by union and agreement relieved, pacified and enriched.

Edward Hall, *Chronicle*, ed. Sir Henry Ellis, London 1809, p. 1.

Julius II's Bull of Dispensation, 26 December 1503

This is a summary of the bull contained in 'The History of the Reformation' written by Bishop Burnet of Salisbury in the reign of

Charles II. The original, like all correspondence to and from the Papacy, was in Latin, and was about three times as long as this summary. This bull was written in 1503, but not published until March 1505.

That the pope, according to the greatness of his authority, having received a petition from prince Henry and the princess Catharine, bearing, That whereas the princess was lawfully married to prince Arthur, (which was perhaps consummated by the carnalis copula,) who was dead without any issue, but they, being desirous to marry for preserving the peace between the crowns of England and Spain, did petition his holiness for his dispensation; therefore the pope, out of his care to maintain peace among all catholic kings, did absolve them from all censures under which they might be, and dispensed with the impediment of their affinity, notwithstanding any apostolical constitutions or ordinances to the contrary, and gave them leave to marry; or if they were already married, he confirming it, required their confessor to enjoin them some healthful penance for their having married before the dispensation was obtained.

Gilbert Burnet, *History of the Reformation* (12), ii, p. 35.

document 3
Prince Arthur's Marriage to Catherine of Aragon

This account of the marriage was written anonymously in 1532 in the pamphlet, 'A Glasse of the Truth'. Supporters of the king felt that it was vital to their case to prove that Arthur consummated the marriage. The account given here was widely reported at the time, but obviously pays no attention to Catherine's testimony.

There be many more specialties than these that go near the matter; for some men of great house say, and (as I am informed) depose upon their oath, that Prince Arthur did report himself unto them that he had carnally known her; and that at divers times, to some at one time, to some at another, so that his sayings were many times reiterated; which, methinketh, giveth much greater faith, insomuch that it is not to be thought that all these times he should speak for ostentation and boasting of himself only; for at some time of these it doth appear by attestation of credible folks, whereof some were his servants near about him at that time, that he spake it for mere necessity, demanding and desiring drink incontinently upon his great labours, in the morning very early, to quench his thirst; answering, when the question was asked him, 'Why, sir, and be ye now so dry?' 'Marry, if thou haddest been as often in Spain this night as I have been, I think verily thou wouldest have been much drier.' Another thing there is more which hath a marvellous appearance in it to declare that she should be known by Prince Arthur, and that is this: Incontinent after his death the name of a prince belonged to him that is now our sovereign lord and king, except his brother had children; and so without creation, or any other solemnity, straight way so to be called thereby; which, if it should not so have followed, should have been a mere injury illated by his father to him, without some other marvellous great consideration. So it was, his brother being dead, upon suspicion that she had been with child, and being also certified by the prince's counsel that they and she both thought the same, the name of prince was deferred from our sovereign lord that now is by the space of a month and more, in which time it was likely the truth to be known. And so, methinketh, there can be no more vehement nor almost a plainer trial of her to be known than this, being withal well considered how well advisedly the noble king his father did always proceed in all his acts and deeds. Yea, and a third there is also, whereby it cannot be denied but that this her ostentation and affirmation is nothing true; and that now is evidently proved by an instrument called a brief, which she by herself or her proctor produced in public judgment before the legates in her defence, because our sovereign's counsel found faults in the bull, which were sufficient in law (as lawyers doth affirm), though the Pope might dispense (as he may not indeed) to annihilate and fordo the marriage between the king and her; for where one of the faults which the king's counsel found was, that after the death of Prince Arthur, in suing for dispensation, she attained a bull, whereof the suggestion was not true, being in one place (as it was said) in the bull *Forsan cognitam*, as who saith, 'may fortune knowen'; which maketh a doubt of that thing which she knew well enough before. And thereby it may well be conjectured that she feared to tell the truth, lest that the Pope, perceiving that she had been known by Prince Arthur, would never have dispensed with this latter marriage; or else, indeed, if she had not been known, she needed not to have put in these terms at all.

A Glasse of the Truth 1532, in (**16**), ii, p. 414–15.

document 4

Impression of Henry VIII

This description was given by the Venetian diplomat, Pasqualigo, in 1515 in a dispatch.

His Majesty is the handsomest potentate I ever set eyes on; above the usual height, with an extremely fine calf to his leg, his complexion very fair and bright, with auburn hair combed straight and short, in the French fashion, and a round face so very beautiful, that it would become a pretty woman, his throat being rather long and thick. He was born on the 28th of June, 1491, so he will enter his twenty-fifth year the month after next. He speaks French, English, and Latin, and a little Italian, plays well on the lute and harpsichord, sings from book at sight, draws the bow with greater strength than any man in England, and jousts marvellously. Believe me, he is in every respect a most accomplished Prince; and I, who have now seen all the sovereigns in Christendom, and last of all these two of France and England in such great state, might well rest content, and with sufficient reason have it said to me,
'abi viator, sat tuis oculis debes'.

Rawdon Brown, *Four Years at the Court of Henry VIII*, London 1854, i, 85.

Wolsey and the Star Chamber

Wolsey drafted this letter to Henry VIII, expressing confidence in his ability to keep order through the Court of Star Chamber. It was probably written in 1518.

And for your realm, our Lord be thanked, it was never in such peace nor tranquillity; for all this summer I have had neither of riot, felony, nor forcible entry, but that your laws be in every place indifferently ministered, without leaning of any manner. Albeit, there hath lately, as I am informed, been a fray between Pygot, your serjeant and Sir Andrew Windsor's servants, for the seisin of a ward whereto both they pretend titles; in the which fray one man was slain. I trust at the next term to learn them the law of the Star Chamber, that they shall ware how from thenceforth they shall redress this matter with their hands. They be both learned in the temporal law, and I doubt not good example shall ensue to see them learn the new law of the Star Chamber, which, God willing they shall have indifferently administered to them according to their deserts.

Letters and Papers (**14**), ii, appendix 38, undated, but August 1517 suggested; quoted by Pollard (**100**) who suggests August 1518.

document 6
John Skelton's Satire on Wolsey

John Skelton (1460?–1529) was very critical of the church in his poetry and reserved special venom for Cardinal Wolsey. After the circulation of this poem in 1523, he was forced to take sanctuary at Westminster.

> In the Chancery, where he sits,
> But such as he admits,
> None so hardy to speek!
> He saith, 'Thou hoddipeke,

Thy learning is too lewd,
Thy tongue is not well-thewd
To seek before our Grace!'
And openly, in that place,
He rages and he raves,
And calls them 'cankered knaves'!
Thus royally he doth deal
Under the King's broad seal;
And in the 'Chequer he them checks
In the Star Chamber he nods and becks,
And beareth him there so stout
That no man dare rowt!
Duke, earl, baron, nor lord,
But to his sentence must accord;
Whether he be knight or squire,
All men must follow his desire.
    . . .
Why come ye not to court
To which court?
To the King's court,
Or to Hampton Court?
Nay, to the King's court!
The King's court
Should have the excellence
But Hampton Court
Hath the preeminence,
And York's Place,
With my Lord's Grace!
To whose magnificence
Is all the confluence,
Suits and supplications,
Embassades of all nations.

John Skelton, Why come ye not to court?

Cromwell's Speech to Parliament 1523

Cromwell prepared and may have delivered this speech criticising the proposed expedition to France. He thought that the king's interests could be best served by the subjugation of Scotland.

I am as desirous that all his most noble enterprises should prosperously go forward as any simple creature that ever was born under his obedience, thinking after my ignorant judgement, that if it would please his magnanimous courage to convert first and chief his whole intent and purpose, not only to the overrunning and subduing of Scotland but also to join the same realm unto his, so that both they and we might live under one law and policy for ever. He should thereby win the highest honour that ever did any noble progenitors since this island was first inhabited, to join unto his noble realm so populous a country, whereby his strength should be of no small part increased and of this act should follow the highest abashment to the said Francis that ever happened to him or any his progenitors before him; not only for that he left the said Scots his ancient allies and which have for his and their sakes provoked our nation so notably heretofore at this time undefended by reason of our sovereign's navy, which he dare not encounter with nor never dare send them succour, so long as he shall know the narrow seas substantially to be kept; but also for such as he shall understand that we have changed our manner of war, which were wont nought else to do but to score the nations about. But when he shall perceive that by the high and politic wisdom of our said most redoubted sovereign, they be joined unto us in one politic body what fear shall we then stand in to lose his possessions without any hope of recovery again. And though it be a common saying that in Scotland is nought to win but strokes, I allege another common saying, who that intendeth France to win, with Scotland let him begin. Which interpreted thus truly, it is but a simpleness for us to think to keep possessions in France, which is severed from us by the ocean sea and suffer Scotland, joined unto us by nature all in one island, unto which we may have recourse at all times when we will, which also to subdue, God being indifferent, lieth ever in our hand, to live under another policy and to recognise another Prince. Send God that our most redoubted sovereign may conquer Scotland, which when we have once joined unto our policy, as a member by nature descending upon the whole, when shall we thereby have the experience how to win and keep other possessions of our most redoubted sovereign of due right and inheritance belonging to his noble crown, which we have in the parts beyond the sea, in which enterprises I beseech God send our most dear and most redoubted sovereign prosperous succession and fortunate achieving of all this his noble enterprise.

Letters and Papers (**14**) iii, 2958.

document 8

The Anti-Clericalism of the Reformation Parliament 1529

Edward Hall was a member of the Reformation Parliament and gave an eye witness account of the opening of the Parliament in 1529. In the absence of any records of the House of Commons for this period, he is a very important source for parliamentary activity during the reign.

When the commons were assembled in the nether house they began to commune of their griefs wherewith the spirituality had before time grievously oppressed them, both contrary to the law of the realm and contrary to all right, and in especial they were sore moved with six great causes:

1. First for the excessive fines which the ordinaries took for probates of Testaments, insomuch that Sir Henry Guilford, knight of the garter and controller of the king's house declared in the open parliament of his fidelity that he and others being executors to Sir William Compton, knight, paid for the probate of his will to the Cardinal and the archbishop of Canterbury a thousand marks sterling. After this declaration, were shewed so many extortions, done by ordinaries for probate of wills, that it were too much to rehearse.

2. The second cause was, that great polling, and extreme exaction which the spiritual men used in making of corps, presents or mortuaries; for the children of the dead should all die for hunger and go a begging, rather than they would of charity give to them the filly cow, which the dead man ought, if he had but only one; such was the charity of them.

3. The third cause was that priests being surveyors, stewards and officers to bishops, abbots and other spiritual heads, had and occupied farms, granges and grazing in every country so that the poor husbandmen could have nothing but of them; and yet for that they should pay dearly.

4. The fourth cause was that abbots, priors and spiritual men kept tan, houses and bought and sold wool, cloth, and all manner of merchandise, as other temporal merchants did.

5. The fifth cause was because the spiritual persons promoted to great benefices, and having their livings of their flocks, were lying in the court in lords houses and took all of their parishioners and nothing spent on them at all; so for that lack of residence, both the poor of the parish lacked refreshing, and universally all the parishioners lacked preaching and true instructions of God's word, to the great peril of their souls.

6. The sixth cause was, because one priest being a little learned, had ten or twelve benefices, and was resident on none; and many well learned scholars in the university, which were able to preach and teach, had neither benefice nor exhibition.

These things before this time might in no wise be touched nor yet talked of by no man except he would be made a heretic, or lose all that he had, for the bishops were chancellors, and had all the rule about the king, so that no man dared once presume to attempt anything contrary to their profit or commodity.

Edward Hall, *Henry VIII* (9), ii, 165–7.

document 9

Wolsey's Account of His Service to the King

These words were said just before Wolsey's death in 1530 according to George Cavendish, Wolsey's gentleman usher. They show the usual lack

*of recrimination of fallen ministers towards the king and they also give
some idea of Henry's strength of will.*

'Well, well, Master Kingston,' quod he, 'I see the matter
against me how it is framed. But if I had served God as
diligently as I have done the King, he would not have given me
over in my grey hairs. Howbeit this is the just reward that I
must receive for my worldly diligence and pains that I have had
to do him service, only to satisfy his vain pleasures, not regard-
ing my godly duty. Wherefore I pray you with all my heart to
have me most humbly commended into his royal majesty,
beseeching him in my behalf to call to his most gracious
remembrance all matters proceeding between him and me from
the beginning of the world unto this day, and the progress of
the same. And most chiefly in the weighty matter yet depending
(meaning the matter newly begun between him and good
Queen Catherine)—then shall him conscience declare whether
I have offended him or no. He is sure a prince of royal courage,
and hath a princely heart; and rather than he will either miss
or want any part of his will or appetite, he will put the loss of
one half of his realm in danger. For I assure you I have often
kneeled before him in his privy chamber on my knees the space
of an hour or two to persuade him from his will and appetite;
but I could never bring to pass to dissuade him therefrom.
Therefore, Master Kingston, if it chance hereafter you to be one
of his privy council (as for your wisdom and other qualities ye
be meet so to be) I warn you to be well advised and assured
what matter ye put in his head; for ye shall never pull it out
again.'

George Cavendish, *Life and Death of Cardinal Wolsey* (**1**), 183–4.

document 10
The Supplication Against the Ordinaries 1532

*Edward Hall describes the presentation of the Supplication by a deputa-
tion from the House of Commons and records the king's speech in reply.
The bill concerning wards and primer seisin is the Bill of Uses.
Ordinaries are clergymen.*

The xviii day of March the Commons' Speaker accompanied with divers knights and burgesses of the Common House came to the King's presence, and there declared to him how the temporal men of his realm were sore aggrieved with the cruel demeanour of the prelates and ordinaries, which touched both their bodies and goods, all which griefs, the Speaker delivered to the King in writing, most humbly beseeching his grace to take such an order and direction in that case, as to his high wisdom might seem most convenient. Further he beseeched the King to consider what pain, charge and cost, his humble subjects of the nether house had sustained since the beginning of this Parliament, and that it would please his grace of his princely benignity to dissolve his court of Parliament, that his subjects might repair into their countries.

When the King had received the Supplication of the Commons, he paused a while and then said: It is not the office of a King which is a judge to be to light of credence, nor I have not, nor will not use the same: for I will hear the party that is accused speak before I give any sentence: your book contains diverse articles of great and weighty matters, and as I perceive, it is against the spiritual persons and prelates of our realm, of which thing you desire a redress and a reformation, which desire and request is more contrariant to your last petition: for you desire to have the parliament dissolved and to depart into your countries, and yet you would have a reformation of your griefs with all diligence. Although that your pain hath been great in tarrying, I assure you mine hath been no less than yours, and yet all the pain that I take for your wealths is to me a pleasure. Therefore, if you will have a profit of your complaint, you must tarry the time, or else to be without remedy. I much commend you that you will not contend nor stand in strife with the spiritual men, which be your Christian brethren, but much more me thinketh that you should not contend with me that am your sovereign Lord and King, considering that I seek peace and quietness of you. For I have sent to you a bill concerning wards and primer seisin, in the which things I am greatly wronged. Wherefore I have offered you reason as I think, yea, and so thinketh all the lords, for they have set their hands to the book. Therefore, I assure you, if you will search out the extremity of the law and then will I not offer you so much again. With this answer, the Speaker and the company departed.

Edward Hall, *Henry VIII* (9), ii, 202–3.

document 11

The Submission of the Clergy

This is a copy of the last form of Submission, which the king required of the clergy dated 15 May 1532. In 1534, an Act for the Submission of the Clergy gave these clauses statutory authority. The commission of thirty-two persons was never appointed.

We your most humble subjects, daily orators, and bedemen of your clergy of England, having our special trust and confidence in your most excellent wisdom, your princely goodness, and fervent zeal to the promotion of God's honour and Christian religion; and also in your learning far exceeding, in our judgment, the learning of all other kings and princes that we have read of; and doubting nothing but that the same shall still continue and daily increase in your majesty.

First do offer and promise *in verbo sacerdotii* here unto your highness, submitting ourselves most humbly to the same, that we will never from henceforth presume to attempt, allege, claim or yet put in use, or to enact, promulgate or execute any canons, constitution or ordinance provincial, or by any other name whatsoever they may be called in our convocation in time coming; which convocation is always, hath been and must be assembled only by your high commandment of writ; unless your highness by your royal assent shall license us to make, promulgate and execute the same, and thereto give your most royal assent and authority.

Secondly, that whereas diverse constitutions and canons provincial, which hath been heretofore enacted, be thought to be not only much prejudicial to your prerogative royal; but also overmuch onerous to your highness' subjects, it be committed to the examination and judgment of thirty-two persons, whereof sixteen to be of the upper and nether house of the temporalty, and other sixteen of the clergy, all to be chosen and appointed by your highness. So that finally whichsoever of the said constitutions shall be thought and determined by the most part of the said thirty-two persons worthy to be abrogated and annulled, the same to be afterwards taken away by your most noble grace and the clergy, and to be abolished as of no force and strength.

Thirdly, that all other of the said constitutions and canons being viewed and approbate by the foresaid thirty-two persons, which by the most part of their judgments do stand with God's laws and your highness', to stand in full strength and power, your grace's most royal assent once impetrate and fully given to the same.

From N. Pocock, *Records of the Reformation* (**16**), ii, 257–8.

King Arthur and Emperor Constantine

This extract shows that the Duke of Norfolk was trying to justify Henry's imperial jurisdiction against that of the Pope from the evidence of history. He also discusses with Chapuys the results to be expected from a General Council of the Church.

... I also said that your Majesty and the Queen had more occasion to be dissatisfied with the Pope in this affair than the King had, whom he has gratified as much as he could. The Duke, referring to the Council, said that the Pope might not get much benefit from it. I said they themselves, though they did not know it, had been partly the cause why the Pope had not so readily consented to the Council, that he might justify himself for various calumnies they had published about him and show that he had given no occasion to the King to do anything against him or the Church, and that his Holiness acted like a good pastor, who instead of being judge of all the world, wished to submit to all the world's judgement.

112

The Duke answered that the Pope had no jurisdiction, except in matters of heresy . . . the Duke said he had lately shown the king of France the seal on the tomb of King Arthur (I did not know of whom he spoke) in which there was a writing, which I would see in a bill of parchment, which he took out of his purse, saying, that he had it copied out for me. This bill contained only the words '*Patricius Arcturus, Britanniae, Galliae, Germaniae, Daciae Imperator*' I said I was sorry he was not also called Emperor of Asia, and that he had not left this King as his successor. . . .

. . . The Duke said that two days ago he was informed that the Pope had, at the solicitation of the Queen's friends, sent them some very injurious mandates, which if the Pope himself came to execute in person, nothing would save him from the fury of the people. He therefore begged me if they came into my hands, to do nothing to execute them. He then said that the Pope in former times had tried to usurp authority and that the people would not suffer it—still less would they do so now; that the King had a right of Empire and recognised no superior; that there had been an Englishman who had conquered Rome, to wit, Brennus; that Constantine had reigned here and the mother of Constantine was English etc. I thanked the Duke for his good will in telling me this, and said my curiosity had not led me to inquire into their affairs or constitutions, which I consider did not bind the minister of your Majesty.

Letters and Papers (**14**), 4513 Jan. 1531. Chapuys to Charles V. Vienna Archives.

document 13
The Act in Restraint of Appeals, 1533

The preamble of this Act is a justification and definition of royal supremacy which was drafted with great care by Thomas Cromwell. The 'sundry ordinaries, laws, statutes and provisions' referred to are the Statutes of Provisors and the Statutes of Praemunire.

Where by divers sundry old authentic histories and chronicles it is manifestly declared and expressed that this realm of

England is an empire, and so hath been accepted in the world, governed by one supreme head and king having the dignity and royal estate of the imperial crown of the same, unto whom a body politic, compact of all sorts and degrees of people divided in terms and by names of spiritualty and temporalty, be bounden and owe to bear next to God a natural and humble obedience; he being also institute and furnished by the goodness and sufferance of Almighty God with plenary, whole and entire power, preeminence, authority, prerogative and jurisdiction to render and yield justice and final determination to all manner of folk resiants or subjects within this realm, in all causes, matters, debates and contentions happening to occur, insurge or begin within the limits thereof, without restraint or provocation to any foreign princes or potentates of the world; the body spiritual whereof having power when any cause of the law divine happened to come in question or of spiritual learning, then it was declared, interpreted and shewed by that part of the said body politic called the spiritualty, now being usually called the English Church, which always hath been reputed and also found of that sort that both for knowledge, integrity and sufficiency of number, it hath been always thought and is also at this hour sufficient and meet of itself, without the intermeddling of any exterior person or persons, to declare and determine all such doubts and to administer all such offices and duties as to their rooms spiritual doth appertain. For the due administration whereof and to keep them from corruption and sinister affection the King's most noble progenitors, and the antecessors of the nobles of this realm, have sufficiently endowed the said Church both with honour and possession. And the laws temporal for trial of propriety of lands and goods, and for the conservation of the people of this realm in unity and peace without ravin or spoil, was and yet is administered, and executed by sundry judges and administers of the other part of the said body politic called the temporalty, and both their authorities and jurisdictions do conjoin together in the due administration of justice the one to help the other. And whereas the King his most noble progenitors, and the Nobility and Commons of this said realm, at divers and sundry Parliaments as well in the time of King Edward I, Edward III, Richard II, Henry IV, and other noble kings of this realm, made sundry ordinances, laws, statutes and

114

provisions for the entire and sure conservation of the prerogatives, liberties and preeminences of the said imperial crown of this realm, and of the jurisdictions spiritual and temporal of the same, to keep it from the annoyance as well of the see of Rome as from the authority of other foreign potentates attempting the diminution or violation thereof as often and from time to time as any such annoyance or attempt might be known or espied. And notwithstanding the said good estatutes and ordinances made in the time of the King's most noble progenitors in preservation of the authority and prerogative of the said imperial crown as is aforesaid, yet nevertheless since the making of the said good statutes and ordinances divers and sundry inconveniences and dangers not provided for plainly by the said former acts, statutes and ordinances have risen and sprung by reason of appeals sued out of this realm to the see of Rome, in causes testamentary, causes of matrimony and divorces, right of tithes, oblations and obventions, not only to the great inquietation, vexation, trouble, costs and charges of the King's Highness and many of his subjects and resiants in this his realm, but also to the great delay and let to the true and speedy determination of the said causes, for so much as the parties appealing to the said court of Rome most commonly do the same for the delay of justice; and forasmuch as the great distance of way is so far out of this realm, so that the necessary proofs nor the true knowledge of the cause can neither there be so well known nor the witnesses there so well examined as within this realm, so that the parties grieved by means of the said appeals be most times without remedy.

Statutes of the Realm, iii, 427–428.

document 14

The Sovereignty of Statute

This section of the preamble of the Dispensations Act 1534 assigns no limits to the powers of statute. It does not, however, say more than that statute law has supremacy over human law (extract 1). There is no mention of divine or natural law in the preamble, but limits are set to the dispensing power in the Act (extract 2).

[1] For where this your Grace's realm, recognising no superior under God but only your Grace, hath been and is free from subjection to any man's laws but only to such as have been devised, made and ordained within this realm for the wealth of the same, or to such other as by sufferance of your Grace and your progenitors the people of this your realm have taken at their free liberty by their own consent to be used amongst them, and have bound themselves by long use and custom to the observance of the same, not as to the observance of the laws of any foreign prince, potentate or prelate, but as to the accustomed and ancient laws of this realm originally established as laws of the same by the said sufferance, consents and custom, and none otherwise: It standeth therefore with natural equity and good reason that in all and every such laws human, made within this realm or induced into this realm by the said sufferance, consents and custom, your Royal Majesty and your Lords spiritual and temporal and Commons, representing the whole state of your realm in this your most High Court of Parliament, have full power and authority not only to dispense but also to authorise some elect person or persons to dispense with those and all other human laws of this your realm and with every one of them, as the quality of the persons and matter shall require; and also the said laws and every of them to abrogate, annul, amplify or diminish, as it shall be seen unto your Majesty and the Nobles and Commons of your realm present in your Parliament meet and convenient for the wealth of your realm, as by divers good and wholesome acts of Parliament made and established as well in your time as in the time of your most noble progenitors it may plainly and evidently appear.

[2] Provided always that this act nor any thing or things therein contained shall be hereafter interpreted or expounded that your Grace, your nobles and subjects, intend by the same to decline or vary from the congregation of Christ's Church in any things concerning the very articles of the Catholic Faith or Christendom; or in any other thing declared by Holy Scripture and the word of God necessary for your and their salvations.

Statutes of the Realm, iii, 464–71.

116

The Power of Proclamation

In a letter of Thomas Cromwell to the Duke of Norfolk, 15 July 1535, Cromwell sent a royal proclamation against conveying coin out of the realm. The Council gave their opinion that it should have the same force as a statute.

May it please your grace to be advertised that I have received your letters, perceiving by the contents thereof that the King's highness doth much marvel that I have not advertised your grace what order my Lord Chancellor and others of his Council hath taken concerning the conveyance of coin out of the realm. Sir, according to your gracious commandment upon Tuesday last, Mr Attorney and I both did intimate and declare the King's pleasure unto my Lord Chancellor who immediately sent for my Lord Chief Justice of the King's Bench, the Chief Justice of the Common Pleas, the Chief Baron and Mr Fitz-herbert, Mr Attorney, Mr Solicitor and I being present and the case by my said Lord Chancellor opened, divers opinions there were, but finally it was concluded that all the statutes should be searched to see whether there was any statute or law able to serve for the purpose and if there were, it was thought good, that if it should happen any accident to be, whereby there might be any occasion that the money should be conveyed out of the realm, that then proclamation should be made, grounded upon the said statute, adding thereunto politically certain things for putting the King's subjects and other in more terror and fear. Upon which device, search was made and a good statute found which was made in the fifth year of King Richard II, copy whereof, translated into English, I do send unto your Grace, drawn in manner of a proclamation by the advice of the King's learned Council. But amongst all other things, I moved unto my said Lord Chancellor, my Lord Chief Justice and other, that if in case there were no law nor statute made already for any such purpose, what might the King's Highness by the advice of his Council do to withstand so great a danger, like as your Grace alleged at my being with you. To the which, it was answered by my Lord Chief Justice that the King's Highness, by the advice of his Council, might make proclamations and use all other policies at his pleasure, as well in this case as in any other, like for avoiding any such dangers and that the said proclamations and policies so devised by the King and his Council, for any such purpose, should be of as good effect as any law made by parliament or otherwise, which opinion, I assure your Grace, I was very glad to hear. Whereupon the said statute was drawn in to a copy, in form as a proclamation. I do now send the same to your Grace and thus the Holy Trinity preserve your Grace in long life, good health, with the increase of much honour. At London the xvth day of July.

Thomas Cromwell's *Letters* (**2**) i, 409–10; also in *Letters and Papers* (**14**), viii, 1042.

document 16

The Nationalisation of the Church

The State Paper of 1534 outlines a plan for the nationalisation of most church assets and the institution of a salaried clergy.

Things to be moved for the King's highness for an increase and augmentation to be had for maintenance of his most royal estate, and for the defence of the realm, and necessary to be provided for taking away the excess which is the great cause of the abuses of the Church.

1. That it may be provided by Parliament that the archbishop of Canterbury may have 2,000 marks yearly and not above and that the residue of the possessions of the archbishopric may be made sure to the King and his heirs for the defence of the realm and maintenance of his royal estate.
2. That the archbishop of York may have £1,000 yearly for maintenance of his estate, and the residue to be to the King and his heirs.
3. That every bishop who may dispend more than 1,000 marks yearly may have 1,000 marks and no more assigned to him.
4. That the King may have, for the maintenance of the estate

of supreme head of the Church of England, the first fruits of every bishopric and benefice for one year after the vacation, of whose gift soever it be, and that the first fruits to the Bishop of Norwich may cease, and no longer be paid but to the King.

5. That the King may have, for the maintenance of his royal estate, the lands and possessions of all monasteries of which the number is or of late has been less than a convent, that is, under 13 persons.

6. That in monasteries where the number is above a convent, for every monk being a priest there may be assigned from the possessions of the house 10 marks; for every novice, not being a priest, £5; and to the abbot or governor as much as the whole convent shall have assigned among them all, to keep hospitality and repair the house; the residue to be for the King.

7. In monasteries of women, where the number is above a convent, every nun is to have yearly 5 marks and the abbess or prioress as much as the whole number; the residue for the King.

8. The King to have the moiety and 'halfundele' of the dividend in every cathedral and collegiate church. The other to go to the residencers.

9. The King to have the third of the revenue of every archdeaconry.

10. The Lord of St. John's to have 1,000 marks, and the rest of his possessions to go to the King, and at his death, the whole; and likewise the lands of every commandry at the death of the knights in possession, for the maintenance of the King's estate, defence against invasion and enterprises against Irishmen.

11. Franchises and liberties to any archbishoprics, bishoprics, cathedrals, priories etc. to be annexed to the Crown, court barons and leets only excepted.

Besides this that the king may have for the charges of the present wars, for defence of Ireland, for the making of Dover haven and other fortresses against Scotland:

1. From every spiritual person who may spend £20 or above 4s in the pound in two years.

2. Under £20, 2s in the pound.

3. From temporal persons who may spend £20 or above in land, or are worth £100 in moveable substance, 2s in the pound in two years.

4. From 40s to £20 in land or £5 to £100 in moveable substance 12d in the pound in two years.

5. Strangers to pay double the rates of the temporal subjects.

Letters and Papers (**14**), vii, 1355.

document 17
Bishop Gardiner's 'The Oration of True Obedience'

This tract was published in Latin in 1535 and was subsequently reprinted many times. Gardiner had defended the independence of the Church just before the Submission of the Clergy (1532), but in this work he preaches pure caesaropapism. In the first extract kings must be obeyed as if they were God and in the second, Church and State are one.

(i) Indeed God, according to his exceeding great and unspeakable goodness toward mankind, to increase the abundance of glory in us, whereby he might establish present matter for us, to exercise ourselves godly and thankworthily in substituted men, who being put in authority as his vicegerents, should require obedience, which we do unto them with no less fruit for God's sake, than we should do it (what honour so ever it were) immediately unto God himself.

And in that place he hath set princes, whom as representers of his image unto men, he would have to be reputed in the supreme and most high room and to excel among all other human creatures at St Peter writeth: and that the same princes reign by his authority, as the holy Proverbs make report. By me (saith God) Kings reign, insomuch that after Paul's saying whosoever resisteth power resisteth the ordinance of God.

(ii) For I am not ignorant of the force of both the manner of speeches and that this word (Church) signifieth not every congregation ... but only that multitude of people, which being united in the profession of Christ, is grown into one body. For this came in by custom, that this term 'church' which else is a common term, became (notwithstanding) the proper name of a more excellent body. But this word (realm) is more plainly known and comprehendeth all subjects of the king's dominions, whosoever they be and of what condition so ever they be, whether they be Jews, barbarians, Saracens, Turks or Christians. Then seeing in this matter, which I have in hand, the matter that is meant by it, is of such sort, that is, agreeth indifferently with both manner of speeches, and seeing the Church of England consisteth of the same sorts of people at this day, that are comprised in this word 'realm', of whom the king is called the head: shall he not being called the head of the realm of England be also the head of the same men when they are named the Church of England?

Janelle, *Obedience in Church and State* (**7**), pp. 89 and 93.

document 18
Cromwell's Injunction to the Clergy 1538

This is the opening of Cromwell's Injunction to the Clergy, 5 September 1538, which ordered the clergy to set up an English Bible in every church. It begins with a list of the King's titles.

IN THE NAME OF GOD AMEN By the authority and commission of the most excellent prince Henry by the grace of God King of England and of France, defender of the faith, Lord of Ireland and in earth supreme head under Christ of the Church of England I, Thomas Lord Cromwell, Lord Privy Seal, Vicegerent to the King's said highness for all his jurisdiction ecclesiastical within this realm, do for the advancement of the true honour of Almighty God, increase of virtue and discharge of the King's Majesty give and exhibit unto you these injunctions following to be kept observed and fulfilled upon the pains hereafter declared

First that ye shall truly observe and keep all and singular the King's highness injunctions given unto you heretofore in my name by his grace's authority, not only upon the pains therein expressed but also in your default now after this second monition continued upon further punishment to be straitly extended towards you by the King's highness arbitrement or his vicegerent aforesaid.

Item that ye shall provide on this side the feast of All Saints next coming, one book of the Holy Bible of the largest volume in English, and the same set up in some convenient place within the said church that ye have care of, where your parishioners may most commodiously resort to the same and read it. The charges of which book shall be ratably borne between you the parson and the parishioners aforesaid, that is to say the one half by you and the other half by them. . . .

Thomas Cromwell, *Letters* (**2**), ii, 151–2.

document 19

The Burning of One Collins at London 1538

This extract from Foxe's 'Book of Martyrs' shows the extreme desire to maintain orthodoxy in the bishopric of London in the years immediately after the political Reformation. The Bishop of London from 1530 to 1539 was John Stokesley.

Neither is here to be omitted the burning of one Collins, some-time a lawyer and a gentleman, which suffered the fire this year also in Smithfield, anno 1538. Whom although I do not recite as in the number of God's professed martyrs, yet nor do I think him to be clean sequestered from the company of the Lord's saved flock and family, notwithstanding that the Bishop of Rome's church did condemn and burn him for an heretic: but rather do recount him therefore as one belonging to the holy company of Saints. At leastwise this case of him and of his end may be thought to be such, as may well reprove and condemn their cruelty and madness, in burning so without all discretion this man, being mad and distract of his perfect wits, as he then was, by this occasion as here followeth.

This gentleman had a wife of exceeding beauty and comeli-ness, but notwithstanding of so light behaviour and unchaste conditions (nothing correspondent to the grace of her beauty) that she forsaking her husband, which loved her entirely, betook herself unto another paramour. Which thing when he understood, he took it very grievously and heavily, more than reason would. At the last being overcome with exceeding dolor and heaviness, he fell mad, being at that time a student in law in London. When he was thus ravished of his wits, by chance he came into a church, where a priest was saying Mass and was come to the place where they used to hold up and show the Sacrament.

Collins being beside his wits, seeing the priest holding up the Host over his head, and showing it to the people: he in like manner counterfeiting the priest, took up a little dog by the legs and held him over his head, shewing him unto the people. And for this he was by and by brought to examination, and condemned to the fire and was burned, and the dog with him, the same year of our Lord, in the which John Lambert was burned 1538.

John Foxe, *Actes and Monuments* (**6**).

document 20
Quest for Uniformity 1540

Thomas Cromwell spoke to the House of Lords as Lord vicegerent in April 1540 on the question of uniformity and outlined the king's plan for securing it. Five days later Cromwell was created Earl of Essex, two months later he was arrested for high treason, and three months later he was executed.

There was nothing which the king so much desired as a firm union among all his subjects, in which he placed his chief security. He knew there were many incendiaries, and much cockle grew up with the wheat. The rashness and licentiousness of some, and the inveterate superstition and stiffness of others in the ancient corruptions, had raised great dissensions, to the sad regret of all good Christians. Some were called papists, others heretics; which bitterness of spirit seemed the more strange, since now the holy scriptures, by the king's great care of his people, were in all their hands, in a language which they understood. But these were grossly perverted by both sides; who studied rather to justify their passions out of them than to direct their belief by them. The king leaned neither to the right nor to the left hand, neither to the one nor the other party; but set the pure and sincere doctrine of the Christian faith only before his eyes: and therefore was now resolved to have this set forth to his subjects, without any corrupt mixtures; and to have such decent ceremonies continued, and the true use of them taught, by which all abuses might be cut off, and disputes about the exposition of the scriptures cease, that so all his subjects might be well instructed in their faith, and directed in the reverent worship of God: and resolved to punish severely all transgressors, of what sort or side soever they were. The king was resolved, that Christ, that the gospel of Christ, and the truth, should have the victory: and therefore had appointed some bishops and divines to draw up an exposition of those things that were necessary for the institution of a Christian man; who were, the two archbishops, the bishop of London, Durham, Winchester, Rochester, Hereford, and St. David's; and doctors Thirlby, Robertson, Cox, Day, Oglethorp, Redmayn, Edgeworth, Crayford, Symonds, Robins, and Tresham. He had also appointed others to examine what ceremonies should be retained, and what was the true use of them; who were, the bishops of Bath and Wells, Ely, Sarum, Chichester, Worcester, and Llandaff. The king had also commanded the judges, and other justices of the peace, and persons commissioned for the execution of the act formerly passed, to proceed against all transgressors, and punish them according to law. And he concluded with an high commendation of the king, whose due praises, he said, a man of far greater eloquence than himself was, could not fully set forth.

Journal of the House of Lords, quoted in (**12**), i, 438.

The Great Bible

This story told by Strype in his book on Thomas Cranmer reveals a generation gap that made it easier for the young to accept the Bible in English. This story was originally told to John Foxe by the son, William Maldon.

When the King had allowed the Bible to be set forth to be read in all churches, immediately several poor men in the town of Chelmsford in Essex, where his father lived and he was born, bought the New Testament and on Sundays at reading of it in the lower end of the church: many would flock about them to hear their reading: and he among the rest, being then but fifteen years old came every Sunday to hear the glad and sweet tidings of the Gospel. But his father observing it once angrily fetched him away, and would have him say the latin matins with him, which grieved him much. And as he returned at other times to have the Scripture read, his father still would fetch him away. This put him upon the thoughts of learning to read English that so he might read the New Testament himself; which, when he had by diligence effected, he and his father's apprentice bought the New Testament, joining their stocks together, and to conceal it laid it under the bedstraw and read it at convenient times. One night his father being asleep, he and his mother chanced to discourse concerning the crucifix, and kneeling down to it, and knocking on the breast then used, and holding up the hands to it when it came by in procession. This he told his mother was plain idolatry, and against the commandment of God, when He saith: Thou shalt not make any graven image, nor bow down to it, nor worship it. His mother, enraged at him for this, said 'Wilt thou not worship His cross, which was about thee when thou was christened, and must be laid on thee when thou art dead?' In this heat the mother and son went to their beds. The sum of this evening's conference she presently repeats to her husband, which he impatient to learn, and boiling in fury against his son for denying worship to be due to the cross, arose up forthwith, and goes into his son's chamber, and like a mad zealot, taking him by the hair of his head with both his hands, pulled him out of the bed, and whipped him

125

unmercifully. And when the young man bore this beating, as he related, with a kind of joy, considering it was for Christ's sake, and shed not a tear, his father seeing that was more enraged, and ran down and fetched a halter, and put it about his neck, saying he would hang him. At length, with much entreaty of the mother and brother, he left him almost dead.

John Strype, *Cranmer*, Oxford 1847, i, 142.
Quoted by Maynard Smith (49), 343-4.

document 22

Man's Place in Society

These two extracts illustrate two concepts of the commonwealth. The first from William Tyndale is an example of the Tudor doctrine of social conservatism that every person should know and keep his place. Both Tyndale and Thomas Starkey illustrate the contemporary taste for likening society to a body.

[a] Let every man therefore wait on the office wherein Christ hath put him, and therein serve his brethren. If he be of low degree, let him patiently therein abide, till God promote him, and exalt him higher. Let kings and head officers seek Christ in their offices, and minister peace and quietness unto the brethren; punish sin, and that with mercy, even with the same sorrow and grief of mind as they would cut off a finger or joint, a leg or arm, of their own body, if there were such disease in them, that either they must be cut off, or else all the body must perish.

William Tyndale, *Doctrinal Treatises* (ed. H. Walter, Parker Soc. 1848, p. 102, "The Parable of the Wicked Mammon").

[b] *Pole:* First, this is certain: that like as in every man there is a body and also a soul, in whose flourishing and prosperous state both together standeth the weal and felicity of man: so likewise there is in every commonalty, city, and country, as it were, a politic body, and another thing also, resembling the soul of man, in whose flourishing both together resteth also the true common weal. This body is nothing else but the multitude

of people, the number of citizens, in every commonalty, city or country. The thing which is resembled to the soul, is civil order and politic law, administered by officers and rulers. For like as the body in every man receiveth his life by the virtue of the soul, and is governed thereby, so doth the multitude of people in every country receive, as it were, civil life by laws well administered by good officers and wise rulers, by whom they be governed and kept in politic order. Wherefore the one may, as me seemeth, right well be compared to the body, and the other to the soul.

Lupset: This similitude liketh me well.

Thomas Starkey, *Dialogue between Pole and Lupset,* Early English Text Society, Extra Ser. xii, (1871), 45.

document 23

Sovereignty and the Word of God

Henry Brinkelowe was a critic of society towards the end of Henry's reign, writing under the pseudonym of Roderick Mors. This extract gives a clear definition of the limits of passive resistance.

Inasmuch as there is no power but of God, and whensoever any persons be grieved, oppressed, or over yoked, they must resort unto the higher powers for remedy, which be ordained of God only for the same cause; and inasmuch as the Council of Parliament is the head Council of all realms, for, it being done with the consent of the King, what laws soever be made thereby, being not against the Word of God, we be bound to observe them. And though they be against God's Word, yet may we not bodily resist them with any war, violence, or insurrection, under pain of damnation. But now, contrariwise, as we may not resist the power of a prince, even so may we not observe nor walk in his wicked laws, if he make any against God's word, but rather to suffer death; so that we may neither observe them, nor yet violently resist them in that case.

The Complaynt of Roderyck Mors, Early English Text Society (1874),5.

King and Parliament

The king upholds parliamentary privilege in Ferrers's Case, 1542, and admits that his powers when acting with Parliament were far larger than when he acted alone. The Lent session that Holinshed is describing is more likely to be 1542 than the commonly accepted 1543 (31).

The King then being advertised of all this proceeding, called immediately before him the lord chancellor of England and his judges, with the Speaker of the Parliament and other of the gravest persons of the Nether house, to whom he declared his opinion to this effect. First commending their wisdoms in maintaining the privileges of their House (which he would not have to be infringed in any point) he alleged that he, being head of the Parliament and attending in his own person upon the business thereof, ought in reason to have privilege for him and all his servants attending there upon him. So that if the said Ferrers had been no burgess, but only his servant, yet in respect thereof he was to have the privilege as well as any other. 'For I understand,' quoth he, 'that you not only for your own persons but also for your necessary servants, even to your cooks and horsekeepers, enjoy the said privilege. . . . And further we be informed by our judges that we at no time stand so highly in our estate royal as in the time of Parliament, wherein we as head and you as members are conjoined and knit together into one body politic, so as whatsoever offence or injury (during that time) is offered to the meanest member of the House is to be judged as done against our person and the whole Court of Parliament. Which prerogative of the court is so great (as our learned counsel informeth us) as all acts and processes coming out of any other inferior courts must for the time cease and give place to the highest . . .'

Raphael Holinshed, *Chronicles* (**13**), iii, 824–6.

Bishop Gardiner Asked to Define Royal Power

In one of Gardiner's letters to Protector Somerset, written after the death of Henry VIII, Gardiner describes how Cromwell tried to force him to state that the king was above the law.

The Lord Cromwell had once put in the King our late Sovereign Lord's head to take upon him to have his will and pleasure regarded for a law; for that, he said, was to be a very king; and thereupon I was called for at Hampton Court. And as the Lord Cromwell was very stout, 'Come on, my Lord of Winchester,' quoth he (for that conceit he had, whatsoever he talked with me, he knew ever as much as I, Greek or Latin, and all), 'answer the King here,' qoth he, 'but speak plainly and directly, and shrink not, man! Is not that,' quoth he, 'that pleaseth the King, a law? Have ye not there, in the civil laws,' quoth he, 'quod principi placuit, and so forth?' quoth he, 'I have somewhat forgotten it now.' I stood still and wondered in my mind to what conclusion this would tend. The King saw me musing, and with earnest gentleness said, 'Answer him whether it be so or no.' it would not answer my Lord Cromwell, but delivered my speech to the King, and told him, I had read indeed of kings that had their will always received for a law, but, I told him, the form of his reign, to make the laws his will, was more sure and quiet; 'and by this form of government ye be established,' quoth I, 'and it agreeable with the nature of your people. If ye begin a new manner of policy, how it will frame, no one can tell; and how this frameth ye can tell; and I would never advise your Grace to leave a certain for an uncertain.'

Letters of Stephen Gardiner (**8**), 399.

Henry VIII's Last Speech in Parliament

This speech delivered on Christmas Eve 1545, displays the same kind of concern of monarch for subjects that was later displayed by Elizabeth. It helps to explain the great veneration in which Henry was held.

Now, since I find such kindness on your part toward me, I cannot choose but love and favour you, affirming that no prince in the world more favoureth his subjects than I do you, nor no subjects or commons more love and obey their sovereign lord than I perceive you do me, for whose defence my treasure shall not be hidden, nor, if necessity require, my person shall not be unadventured: yet although I with you, and you with me, be in this perfect love and concord, this friendly amity cannot continue, except both you my lords temporal and you, my lords spiritual, and you my loving subjects, study and take pain to amend one thing, which surely is amiss, and far out of order, to the which I most heartily require you; which is that charity and concord is not amongst you, but discord and dissension beareth rule in every place. ... I see and hear daily that you of the clergy preach one against another, teach one contrary to another, inveigh one against another without charity or discretion. Some be too stiff in their old Mumpsimus, other be too busy and curious in their new Sumpsimus. Thus all men almost be in variety and discord, and few or none preach truly and sincerely the word of God according as they ought to do. Shall I now judge you charitable persons doing this? No, no, I cannot do so. Alas, how can the poor souls live in concord when you preachers sow amongst them in your sermons, debate and discord: of you they look for light, and you bring them to darkness. Amend these crimes I exhort you, and set forth God's word, both by true preaching, and good example giving, or else I, whom God hath appointed his Vicar, and high minister here, will see these divisions extinct, and these enormities corrected, according to my very duty, or else I am an unprofitable servant and untrue officer.

Edward Hall, *Henry VIII* (**9**), ii, 355–7.

French Invasion of England 1545

The same month (June 1545) also the Lord Lisle, admiral of England, with the English fleet entered the mouth of the Seine, and came before Newhaven (Le Havre) where a great navy of the Frenchmen lay, to the number of 200 ships and 26 galleys, whereof the pope (as was reported) had sent 20 well furnished with men and money, to the aid of the French King. The Englishmen being not past 160 sail and all ships determined not to set upon the Frenchmen where they lay: ... and so the Englishmen for fear of flats were compelled to enter the main sea and so sailed into Portsmouth where the King lay, for he had knowledge by his spies that the Frenchmen intended to land in the Isle of Wight, wherefore he repaired to that coast, to see his realm defended.

After this, the eighteenth of July, the admiral of France, Monsieur Dombalt hoist up sails, and with his whole navy came forth into the seas, and arrived on the coast of Sussex before Bright Hampstead (Brighton) and set certain of his soldiers on land to burn and spoil the country: but the beacons were fired and the inhabitants thereabouts came down so thick, that the Frenchmen were driven to fly with loss of diverse of their numbers: so that they did little hurt there. Immediately hereupon they made to the point of the Isle of Wight, called St Helens point, and there in good order upon their arrival they cast anchors and sent daily sixteen of their galleys to the very haven of Portsmouth. The English navy lying there in the same haven, made themselves ready, and set out towards the enemy and still the one shot hotly at the other: but the wind was so calm, that the King's ships could bear no sail, which greatly grieved the minds of the Englishmen and made the enemies more bold to approach with their galleys, and to assail the ships with their shot even within the haven.

The twentieth of July, the whole navy of the Englishmen made out and purposed to set on the Frenchmen, but in setting forth, through too much folly, one of the King's ships called the Mary Rose was drowned in the midst of the haven, by reason that she was overladen with ordnance, and had the ports left open, which were very low, and the great artillery unbreached;

so that when the ship should turn, the water entered and suddenly she was sunk. In her was Sir George Carew and 400 soldiers under his guiding. There escaped not passed 40 persons of the whole number. On the morrow after about 2000 of the Frenchmen landed in the Isle of Wight, where one of their chief captains named le Chevalier Daux, a Provencal, was slain with many others and the residue with loss and shame driven back to their galleys.

The King perceiving the great Armada of the Frenchmen to approach, caused the beacons to be fired ... thereupon they repaired to his presence in great numbers well furnished with armour, weapon, victuals, and all other things necessary, so that the Isle was garnished and all the frontiers along the coast fortified with exceeding great multitudes of men. The French captains having knowledge by certain fishermen, whom they took that the King was present, and so huge a power ready to resist them, they disanchored and drew along the coast of Sussex, and a small number of them landed again in Sussex, of whom few returned to their ships.

Raphael Holinshed, *Chronicles* (**13**) iii, 847–8. The original version from which this account was taken can be found in Hall (**9**).

Chronological Summary 1527–47

1491	June 28	Henry born at Greenwich.
1501	Nov. 14	Arthur and Catherine of Aragon married.
1502	Apr. 2	Arthur died.
1505	Mar.	The papal dispensation published.
1509	Apr. 21	Death of Henry VII at Richmond Palace.
	June 11	Henry and Catherine of Aragon married.
	June 24	Coronation.
1527	Feb.	Bishop of Tarbes questioned Mary's legitimacy.
	Mar.	Clement VII annulled Margaret's marriage with Angus.
	May	Rome sacked by Imperial Army.
	June	Henry told Catherine that she was no longer considered his wife.
	July	Wolsey crossed Channel to meet Francis I.
	Oct.	William Knight sent to Rome.
	Dec.	Clement VII escaped to Orvieto.
1528	Mar.	Fox and Gardiner reached Orvieto.
	June	Commission to try case in England conceded. Truce with the Netherlands over trade.
	Sept.	Lautrec's army capitulated at Aversa.
	Oct.	Campeggio arrived in England. Spanish brief discovered.
	Dec.	Clement VII ordered the decretal commission to be destroyed.
1529	May	Court opened at Blackfriars.
	June	Henry and Catherine appear before court. Battle of Landriano: Treaty of Barcelona.
	July	Campeggio adjourned court.
	Nov.–Dec.	Fifth Parliament, 1st session (Reformation Parliament).
1530		Consultation of foreign universities.
	June	Papal court to hear Henry's case at Rome opened.

1530	Nov.	Wolsey died.
	Dec.	Clergy charged with praemunire.
1531	Jan.–Mar.	Second session of Parliament.
	Feb.	Canterbury Convocation pay fine of £100,000.
1532	Jan.–May	Third session of Parliament.
	Mar.	Supplication against the Ordinaries presented to King.
	May	Submission of the Clergy.
		Thomas More resigned as Lord Chancellor.
		Act of Conditional Restraint of Annates (23 Hen. VIII, c.20).
		A Glasse of the Truth published.
	Oct.	Henry met Francis I at Calais.
	Dec.	Anne Boleyn became pregnant.
1533	Jan.	Henry married Anne Boleyn.
	Feb.–Apr.	Fourth session of Parliament.
		Act in Restraint of Appeals (24 Hen VIII c.12).
	May	Cranmer's court opened at Dunstable.
		Negotiations opened with Schmalkaldic League.
	July	Carne and Bennet recalled from Rome.
	Sept.	Elizabeth born.
1534	Jan.–Mar.	Fifth session of Parliament.
		Act in Restraint of Annates (25 Hen VIII c.20).
		Dispensations Act (25 Hen VIII c.21).
		First Succession Act (25 Hen VIII c.22).
	May	Henry made treaty with Lubeck.
		Pope Clement VII died.
	June	Geraldine Rebellion in Ireland began.
	Nov.–Dec.	Sixth session of Parliament.
		Act of Supremacy (26 Hen VIII c.1).
		Act of First Fruits and Tenths (26 Hen VIII c.3).
1535		Publication of *Defensor Pacis* (Marsiglio), *De Vera Obedientia* (Gardiner), *Power of the Clergy* and *Answer to a Letter* (St German).
	June	Fisher executed.
	July	More executed.
	Oct.	Coverdale's Bible published.
1536	Jan.	Catherine of Aragon died.
	Feb.–Apr.	Seventh session of Parliament.
		Statute of Uses (27 Hen VIII c.10).

		Act abolishing certain franchises (27 Hen VIII c.24).
		Act for the shiring of Wales (27 Hen VIII c. 26).
		Dissolution of the Monasteries (27 Hen VIII c.28).
	May	Anne Boleyn beheaded.
		Henry married Jane Seymour.
	June	Sixth Parliament met.
		Second Succession Act (28 Hen VIII c.7).
	July	Ten Articles published.
	Aug.	Cromwell's First Injunctions.
	Oct.	Pilgrimage of Grace.
	Dec.	Free pardon granted to Pilgrims.
1537	Jan.	Bigod Rebellion.
		Council of the North established.
	Oct.	Edward born.
		Jane Seymour died.
1538	June	Truce of Nice.
	July	Charles V, Francis I and the Pope met at Aigues Mortes.
	Aug.	Exeter conspiracy. Geoffrey Pole arrested.
	Sept.	Cromwell's Second Injunctions.
	Dec.	Papal bull of deposition published.
1539	Jan.	Talks opened with Schmalkaldic League in England.
	Feb.	French and Imperial ambassadors leave.
	Mar.	Invasion scare.
	Apr.	Seventh Parliament called.
		Proclamations Act (31 Hen c.8).
		Second Act of Dissolution (31 Hen VIII c.13).
		Act of Six Articles (31 Hen VIII c.14).
		Great Bible published.
1539	Oct.	Marriage Treaty with Cleves.
1540		Court of First Fruits and Tenths and Court of Wards established.
		Privy Council formalised.
	Jan.	Henry married Anne of Cleves.
	Feb.	Charles V crushed Revolt in Ghent.
	July	Marriage with Anne annulled.
		Thomas Cromwell beheaded.

1540	July	Henry married Catherine Howard.
1541	June	Henry made King of Ireland (in Dublin).
	Aug.	Henry went to York for meeting with James V.
1542		Court of General Surveyors established.
	Jan.	Eighth Parliament called.
	Feb.	Catherine Howard executed.
	Mar.	Ferrers' Case (**93**).
	Oct.	War broke out with Scotland.
	Nov.	Battle of Solway Moss.
	Dec.	James V died.
1543	Feb.	Henry allied with Charles V against France.
	Apr.	Earl of Lennox arrived in Scotland.
	May	*King's Book* published.
	July	Henry married Catherine Parr.
		Treaty of Greenwich signed with Scotland.
1544		3rd Succession Act (35 Hen VIII c.1).
	May	Hertford's amphibious attack on Scotland.
	Sept.	Boulogne surrendered.
		Charles and Francis make peace at Crépi.
1545	July	Invasion scare.
	Nov.	9th Parliament met.
1546	May	Cardinal Beaton murdered.
	June	Peace made with France.
	Dec.	Fall of the Howards; Norfolk and Surrey arrested.
1547	Jan.	Surrey executed.
	Jan. 27	Henry VIII died, aged 57, at Westminster.

Bibliography

DOCUMENTS AND CONTEMPORARY ACCOUNTS

1 Cavendish, George, *The Life and Death of Cardinal Wolsey, Two Early Tudor Lives*, R. S. Sylvester and D. P. Harding, Yale University Library 1962.

2 Cromwell, Thomas, *Life and Letters*, ed. R. B. Merriman, Oxford University Press 1902.

3 *Documents Illustrative of English Church History*, ed. H. Gee and W. J. Hardy, 1896.

4 Strype, John, *Ecclesiastical Memorials*, 3 vols, Oxford University Press 1820–40.

5 *English Historical Documents*, vol. V, 1485–1558, ed. C. H. Williams, Eyre & Spottiswoode, 1967.

6 Foxe, John, *Acts and Monuments* (*The Book of Martyrs*), ed. J. Pratt, London, 1870.

7 Gardiner, Stephen, *De Vera Obedientia* printed in Janelle— *Obedience in Church and State*, Cambridge University Press 1930.

8 Gardiner, Stephen, *Letters*, ed. J. A. Muller, Cambridge University Press 1933.

9 Hall, Edward, *Henry VIII*, ed. C. Whibley, 2 vols, London 1904.

10 Harpsfield, Nicholas, *A Treatise on the Pretended Divorce between Henry VIII and Catherine of Aragon*, ed. N. Pocock, Camden Society 1878.

11 Harpsfield, Nicholas, *The Life and Death of Sir Thomas More, knight, Two Early Tudor Lives*, R. S. Sylvester and D. P. Harding, Yale University 1962.

12 Burnet, Gilbert, *History of the Reformation of the Church of England*, ed. N. Pocock, 7 vols, Oxford University Press 1965.

13 Holinshed, Raphael, *Chronicles*, ed. Henry Ellis, 6 vols, London 1807–8.

14 *Letters and Papers, Foreign and Domestic of the Reign of Henry VIII 1509–47*, ed. Brewer, Gairdner and Brodie, 21 vols, 1892–1910.

137

15   *Letters of Henry VIII*, ed. M. St Clare Byrne, Cassell 1968.
16   Pocock, Nicholas, *Records of the Reformation*, 2 vols, Oxford University Press 1870.
17   Skelton, John, *Complete Poems*, Dent 1931.
18   Elton, G. R., *The Tudor Constitution*, Cambridge University Press 1960.
19   *Tudor Royal Proclamations, I: The Early Tudors (1485–1553)*, L. Hughes and J. F. Larkin, Yale University Press 1964.
20   Vergil, Polydore, *The Anglica Historia*, ed. Hay, Camden Society 1950.
21   Wriothesley, Charles, *A Chronicle of England*, ed. Hamilton, Camden Society, 2 vols, 1875–7.

SECONDARY SOURCES

22   Allen, J. W., *A History of Political Thought in the Sixteenth Century*, Methuen 1928.
23   Bagwell, R., *Ireland under the Tudors*, Longmans 1885, reprinted 1963.
24   Baumer, F. le van, *The Early Tudor Theory of Kingship*, Yale University Press 1940.
25   Caspari, F., *Humanism and the Social Order in England*, University of Chicago Press 1954.
26   Chambers, R. W., *Thomas More*, Cape 1935.
27   Constant, G. *The Reformation in England; The English Schism 1509–1547*, Sheed & Ward 1934.
28   Dickens, A. G. *The English Reformation*, Batsford 1964.
29   Dickens, A. G., *Thomas Cromwell and the English Reformation*, English Universities Press 1959.
30   Dietz, F. C., *English Government Finance 1485–1558*, University of Illinois Studies in Social History, 1920.
31   Dodds, M. H. and Dodds, R., *The Pilgrimage of Grace and the Exeter Conspiracy*, Cambridge University Press 1935.
32   Donaldson, G., *Scotland James V to James VII*, Oliver & Boyd 1965.
33   Elton, G. R., *England under the Tudors*, Methuen 1955.
34   Elton, G. R., *The Tudor Revolution in Government*, Cambridge University Press 1953.
35   Fletcher, A., *Tudor Rebellions*, Longmans 1968 (Seminar Studies in History).

138

36   Hexter, J. H., *Reappraisals in History*, Longmans 1961.
37   Holdsworth, W. S., *A History of English Law*, vol. iv, Methuen, third edition 1945.
38   Hoskins, W. G., *Essays in Leicestershire History*, Liverpool 1950.
39   Hume Brown, P., *History of Scotland*, vol. i, Cambridge University Press 1899.
40   Kerridge, E., *Agrarian Problems in the Sixteenth Century and After*, Allen & Unwin 1969.
41   Knowles, D., *The Religious Orders in England*, vol. iii, Cambridge University Press 1959.
42   Lehmburg, S. E., *The Reformation Parliament*, Cambridge 1970.
43   Lockyer, R., *Henry VII*, Longmans 1968 (Seminar Studies in History).
44   McConica, J. K., *English Humanists and Reformation Politics*, Oxford University Press 1965.
45   Mackie, J. D., *The Earlier Tudors*, Oxford University Press 1952 (Oxford History of England).
46   Marcus, G. J., *A Naval History of England I: The Formative Years*, 1961.
47   Mattingly, G., *Catherine of Aragon*, Cape 1950.
48   Mattingly, G., *Renaissance Diplomacy*, Cape 1955.
49   Maynard Smith, H., *Henry VIII and the Reformation*, Macmillan 1948.
50   Muller, J. A., *Stephen Gardiner and the Tudor Reaction*, Macmillan New York 1926.
51   Neale, J. E., *Elizabeth and her Parliaments*, Cape 1953.
52   Pickthorn, K. W. M., *Early Tudor Government*, vol. ii: *Henry VIII*; 2nd edn, Cambridge University Press 1951.
53   Pollard, A. F., *Factors in Modern History*, Constable 1907.
54   Pollard, A. F., *Henry VIII*, Longmans 1951 edn.
55   Pollard, A. F., *The Evolution of Parliament*, Longmans 1926.
56   Pollard, A. F., *Wolsey*, Longmans 1929; Fontana Library 1965 with introd. by G. R. Elton.
57   Powicke, M., *The Reformation in England*, Oxford University Press 1941.
58   Raab, F., *The English Face of Machiavelli*, Routledge & Kegan Paul 1964.
59   Ramsey, P., *Tudor Economic Problems*, Gollancz 1963.
60   Richardson, W. C., *Tudor Chamber Administration 1485–1547*, Louisiana State University Press 1952.

61 Ridley, J., *Thomas Cranmer*, Oxford University Press 1962.

62 Scarisbrick, J. J., *Henry VIII*, Eyre & Spottiswoode 1968.

63 Scott Thomson, G., *Lords Lieutenant in the Sixteenth Century*, Longmans 1923.

64 Simon, Joan, *Education & Society in Tudor England*, Cambridge University Press 1966.

65 Slavin, A. J., ed. *The 'New Monarchies' and Representative Assemblies: Mediaeval Constitutionalism or Modern Absolutism?* Boston, Heath 1965 (Problems in European Civilisation).

66 Smith, R. B., *Land and Politics in the England of Henry VIII*, Oxford University Press 1970.

67 Sturge, C., *Cuthbert Tunstall*, Longmans 1938.

68 Thirsk, Joan, ed. *The Agrarian History of England & Wales, Vol. IV 1500–1640*, Cambridge University Press 1967.

69 Ullmann, W., *Principles of Government and Politics in the Middle Ages*, Methuen 1961.

70 Wernham, R. B., *Before the Armada*, Cape 1966.

71 Wickson, R., *The Community of the Realm in Thirteenth Century England*, Longman 1970 (Seminar Studies in History).

72 Woodward, G. W. O., *The Dissolution of the Monasteries*, Blandford 1966.

73 Zeeveld, W. G., *Foundations of Tudor Policy*, Methuen 1948.

ARTICLES, ESSAYS AND PAMPHLETS

The following abbreviations are used:

BIHR Bulletin of the Institute of Historical Research
EHR   English Historical Review
HJ   Historical Journal
JEH   Journal of Ecclesiastical History
PP   Past and Present
TRHS Transactions of the Royal Historical Society.

74 Brock, R. E., 'The Early Tudor courtier in society: summary of thesis', *BIHR* 37, 1964

75 Brooks, F. W., 'The Council of the North', *Historical Association Pamphlet* G.25; rev. edn 1966.

76 Cooper, J. P., 'A revolution in Tudor history?' *PP* 26, 1963.

77 Davies, C. S. L., 'A new life of Henry VIII', *History* 54, 1969.

78 Elton, G. R., 'A revolution in Tudor History' *PP* 32, 1965.

79 Elton, G. R., 'Henry VIII. An essay in revision', *Historical Association Pamphlet* G.51, 1962.

80 Elton, G. R., 'Henry VIII's Act of Proclamations', *EHR* 75, 1960.

81 Elton, G. R., 'King or minister? The man behind the Henrician Reformation', *History* 39, 1954.

82 Elton, G. R., 'The political creed of Thomas Cromwell', *TRHS* 6, 1956.

83 Elton, G. R., 'The Tudor Revolution: a reply', *PP* 29, 1964.

84 Harriss, G. L., 'A revolution in Tudor history', *PP* 25, 1963, and *PP* 31, 1965.

85 Hay, D., 'The early Renaissance in England', in *Essays presented to Garrett Mattingly*, Cape 1966.

86 Heinze, R. W., 'The pricing of meat. A study in the use of Royal Proclamations in the reign of Henry VIII', *HJ* 12, 1969.

87 Hurstfield, J. ,'Was there a Tudor despotism after all?' *TRHS* 17, 1966.

88 Hurstfield, J., 'The revival of feudalism in early Tudor England', *History* 37, 1952.

89 Ives, E. W., 'Common lawyers in Pre-Reformation England', *TRHS* 18, 1967.

90 Kelly, M., 'The submission of the clergy', *TRHS* 15, 1965.

91 Koebner, R., 'Imperial crown of this realm, Henry VIII, Constantine the Great, and Polydore Vergil', *BIHR* 26, 1953.

92 Lehmburg, S. E., 'Supremacy and viceregency: a re-examination', *EHR* 81, 1966.

93 Leonard, H. H., 'Ferrers' case: a note', *BIHR* 42, 1969.

94 Levine, M., 'Henry VIII's use of spiritual and temporal jurisdictions', *HJ* 10, 1967.

95 Miller, Helen, 'Attendance in the House of Lords in the reign of Henry VIII', *HJ* 10, 1967.

96 Miller, Helen, 'London and Parliament in the reign of Henry VIII', *BIHR* 35, 1965.

97 Parker, T. M., 'Was Thomas Cromwell a Machiavellian?' *JEH* 1950.

98 Pollard, A. F., 'The Council under the Tudors', EHR 37, 1922.

99 Pollard, A. F., 'The Privy Council under the Tudors', *EHR*, 38, 1923.

141

100 Pollard, A. F., 'The Star Chamber under the Tudors', *EHR* 37, 1922.

101 Wernham, R. B., 'Review of Elton's Tudor revolution in government', *EHR* 71, 1956.

102 Williams, P., 'The Tudor state', *PP* 25, 1963.

Index

Index

Index